I0406060

Gold

Understanding, truth & profit.

By Momanyi Bichanga

Gold begets in brethren hate;

Gold in family's debate;

Gold does friendship separate;

Gold does civil wars create.

Abraham Cowley

CONTENTS

Why gold?

"Gold is money. Everything else is credit".   J. P. Morgan

Gold, like no other metal, has a fascinating history and a special place in the world. For thousands of years it has been used as an ornament of kings, a currency and standard for global currencies, in competitions as symbol of victory and more recently, in a wide range of electronic devices and medical applications. Ancient civilizations used gold for the decoration of tombs and temples. In modern days FMI and WB suggested the use of gold as monetary reference, i.e., the value of a bill guarantees a given amount of gold. In sports the winner gets a gold medal. Other example of gold as symbol of power, health and prosperity is the gold mirror fish Mercedes Benz C63 AMG (Image 1). Although there are doubts whether the car is simple paint or real gold paint, it already arose many debates about expending big amount of money on the beautification of such car.

Why is gold so valuable?

First, it is important to remember some basic concepts about gold. Gold is a dense, soft, shiny, malleable, and ductile metal. It is a chemical element with the symbol Au and atomic number 79. Its symbol is Au. The melting point of gold is 1,948°F (1,064°C) and its Boiling point is 5,173°F (2,856°C). The atomic mass of gold is 196.96657 ± 0.00004 u. The density of gold is 19.30 g cm-3. Some possible reasons for its high value are its unique aesthetic and special properties.

Color and aesthetic

The symbol of gold is Au, from the greek word aurum, which means glow of sunshine. The English word gold comes from the words gulb and ghel referring also to the color. It is the only metal of this color. The gold's characteristic yellow color is due to the arrangement of its electrons. When alloyed with other metals like silver and cooper it has different colors, according to the percentages of the alloy (Image of gold alloys).

Physical and chemical properties

Use Gold has unique physical chemical characteristics that made it very valuable. Gold is the most malleable and ductile of all the metals. One ounce of gold can be drawn into more than 80 Km of thin gold wire. One ounce of gold can be beaten into a sheet covering 9 square meters and 0.000018 cm thick. Gold has an electrical resistivity of 0.022 micro-ohm and a thermal conductivity of 310 W m-1. Hence, it is very efficient for the transmission of heat and electricity. Gold has the highest corrosion resistance of all the metals and it is corroded only by a mixture of nitric and hydrochloric acid. Gold is a noble metal because it does not oxidize.

Scarcity

The mentioned characteristics are enough to make a very useful and desired metal; thus, a very valuable one. Besides, it is important to consider that gold is rather scarce. It is estimated that the whole gold of the planet equals a total of 168,180 tons or 5,407,112,558 ounces. To visualize this volume, let's imagine a single solid gold cube with edges of about 19 meters. This is about three meters shorter than the length of a tennis court.

The Fever

In order to understand the significance of the Gold Rush, it is important to look back at the events that led to the discovery of gold in California. One of the most important events was the Mexican-American War (1846-48). The Mexican-American War was a war of national aggression to gain territory. It followed the 1845 annexation of Texas, which Mexico regarded as its territory. In 1836 the Texian Army won the Battle of San Jacinto against Mexican forces, led by famed general Santa Anna, and the Republic of Texas declared its independence from Mexico.

But Mexico had refused to acknowledge this action and warned the U.S. that if it tried to make Texas part of the U.S., Mexico would declare war. In 1845 Texas voluntarily asked to join the U.S. and became the 28th state. This action led to Mexico to declare war on the United States, starting the Mexican-American War.

After a series of conflicts spanning two years, the United States won the war. When the dust settled, the U.S. had gained a significant amount of new territory. The region collectively known as the Mexican Cession included all present-day California, Texas, Colorado, Arizona, New Mexico, Nevada, and Utah. The signing of the Treaty of Guadalupe-Hidalgo officially ended the war on February 2, 1848. In addition to the ceded territory, Mexico gave up its claims on Texas and recognized the Rio Grande River as America's southern border.

At the time, the war was regarded as a major American victory over a hostile foe, but in the wake of the sectional strife of the Civil War the Mexican-American War was all but forgotten by history. But the war was pivotal in shaping our nation's future. It cemented the idea of the United States as an expansionist, transcontinental empire. It fulfilled the nation's vision of, Manifest Destiny – creating one nation from Atlantic to Pacific. It shaped the land on which many Americans live today. And it led directly to the California Gold Rush.

Unbeknownst to both the United States and Mexico at the time, the Treaty of Guadalupe-Hidalgo would serve to further America's growing wealth and prestige. For just six days before the treaty was signed, gold was discovered in the foothills of the Sierra Nevada Mountains in California. None of the delegates at the signing of the treaty could have imagined that the rivers and streams in California were soon to yield a fortune in gold.

In reality, neither the United States nor Mexico thought much of California. The land in California was a dangerous, semi-arid wilderness, inhabited with native tribes. The war had simply been about borders and territory – not what the territory actually held. Pioneers and migrants were more likely to choose the fertile territory of Oregon than they were California.

Gold was discovered on January 24, 1848 by John W. Marshall, a carpenter and sawmill operator who worked at Sutter's Mill, owned by pioneer and German-born immigrant John Sutter. During his early morning routine check of the water-powered sawmill, Marshall spotted a glint of gold beneath the surface of the South Fork American River. Marshall plucked the peasized particle from the water and recalled, "I reached my hand down and picked it up; it made

my heart thump, for I was certain it was gold." Marshall took his discovery to Sutter, who used an encyclopedia to confirm the find. Sutter recalled the even years later in a magazine:

It was a rainy afternoon when Mr. Marshall arrived at my office in the Fort, very wet. . . .

He told me then that he had some important and interesting news which he wished to communicate secretly to me, and wished me to go with him to a place where we should not be disturbed, and where no listeners could come and hear what we had to say. I went with him to my private rooms . . . I forgot to lock the doors, and it happened that the door was opened by the clerk just at the moment when Marshall took a rag from his pocket, showing me the yellow metal; he had about two ounces of it. . . . After [reading] the long article "gold" in the Encyclopedia Americana, I declared this to be gold of the finest quality, of at least 23 carats.

Sutter swore his workers to secrecy, but within months the secret was out, and the Gold Rush was on.

Newspaper reports on the discovery were initially met with disbelief, but once evidence of gold was brought into San Francisco the frenzy began. The San Francisco-based journal, The Californian, published the following on May 29,

1848:

'The whole country from San Francisco to Los Angeles, and from the sea shore to the base of the Sierra Nevada, resounds with the sordid cry of gold! GOLD!! GOLD!!! – while the field is left half planted, the house half built, and everything neglected but the manufacture of shovels and pickaxes.'

The rush

By mid-June 1848, three-quarters of San Francisco's male population had left the city for the foothills of the Sierra Nevada in search of gold. All of Sutter's workmen abandoned him to seek their fortunes in the rivers and streams, gripped with "gold fever Sutter complained that "even my cook has left me." The Gold Rush turned life upside down." When the news of gold reached the East coast, many men who had trained as bankers, lawyers, and doctors in the East now

migrated westward, spending their days knee-deep in freezing water, moving rocks and stones until their hands were numb searching for gold.

One man likened the "gold fever" to a highly contagious disease. Writing to his friends on the East coast he said, "The whole population are going crazy . . . Old as well as young are daily falling victim to the gold fever." Wives and families were abandoned, left behind to figure out ways to support themselves. Shops were boarded up. Schools were closed. Soldiers abandoned their posts. Benjamin Kloozer, a soldier stationed in California, was torn between duty to his country and the lure of gold. As a soldier his wages were six dollars a month, but mining for gold he stood to make as much as $150 per day. Writing to his brother in Boston, he detailed his predicament, "I hate to desert . . . I am almost crazy. . . . Excuse this letter, as I have the 'gold fever' shockingly bad."

Not all Americans viewed the Gold Rush as a positive occurrence for the country. Literary greats

Ralph Waldo Emerson and Henry David Thoreau spoke out on the detrimental effects of the event. Emerson wrote, "It was a rush and a scramble or needy adventurers, and, in the western country, a general jail-delivery of all the rowdies of the rivers."

Thoreau went further in his denunciation of the gold seekers, writing:

The recent rush to California and the attitude of the world, even or its philosophers and prophets, in relation to it appears to me to reflect the greatest disgrace on mankind.

That so many are ready to get their living by the lottery of gold-digging without contributing any value to society, and that the great majority who stay at home justify them in this both by precept and example! . . . Going to California. It is only three thousand miles nearer to hell. . . . Did God direct us so to get our living, digging where we never planted, and He would perchance reward us with lumps of gold? It is a text, oh! for the Jonah's of this generation, and yet the pulpits are silent. The gold of California is a touchstone which has betrayed the rottenness, the baseness, of mankind. Satan, from one of his elevations, showed mankind the kingdom of California, and they entered into a compact with him at once. (Thoreau journal February 1, 1852)

Arrival of the Forty-niners

The discovery of gold in 1848 by James Marshall sparked a massive wave of westward migration. The largest influx occurred in 1849, and those prospectors who sought their fortunes became known collectively as forty-niners, in reference to the year they arrived. Fortune seekers came by land and sea, from every corner of the world. There were three ways to journey to California in the days of the Gold Rush. By far the easiest and most popular route was the "Panama shortcut." This journey was 7,000 miles and took approximately two to three months. Gold seekers would sail down the eastern coast of the United States to Panama.

There they faced a thirty-five mile overland journey through the jungle, cutting across the Isthmus of Panama to reach the waters of the Pacific Ocean. They then boarded another ship which took them north along the western coast of Mexico to San Francisco. As California's major port city, San Francisco became the gateway to gold.

The second route was also by sea. Although it was the longest in terms of distance, nearly 15,000 miles, it was also the safest route, despite the risk of high waves, frigid temperatures, and a lack of fresh food. Travelers would sail south from the U.S. east coast past South America, down around the tip of Cape Horn, and back north through the Pacific Ocean to California. This route took approximately four to eight months.

The third and most treacherous route was by land – cutting across the continental United States by wagon train. The shortest in terms of distance – only 3,000 miles – the overland journey could take three to seven months. Traveling by ship was costly, so for many this was the only viable option. Travelers feared attacks from American Indians and wildlife, but the biggest threat actually came from diseases and sicknesses such as cholera, diphtheria, "mountain fever" (similar to typhoid), and pneumonia. The hardships that were encountered were numerous; belongings were lost crossing rivers, wagons broke down after encountering barely cleared trails, pack animals dropped dead from exhaustion, and weather ranging from violent thunderstorms and torrential rain to dust storms and scorching heat plagued gold seekers.

In 1849, San Francisco's population skyrocketed from 812 to 20,000 people. The cost of land soared – the same plot of land which had cost $16 in 1847, sold for $45,000 just eighteen months later. Prices of goods and commodities also rose. Fresh produce was in high demand,with apples selling for $5 each and a dozen eggs for $50.

Carlifornia

In California, the Gold Rush became the largest mass migration in American history since it brought about 300,000 people to California. It all started on January 24, 1848, when James W. Marshall found gold on his piece of land at Sutter's Mill in Coloma. The news of gold quickly spread around. People from Oregon, Sandwich Islands (now Hawaii) and Latin America were the first to hear the breaking news, so they were the first to arrive in order to test their luck in California by the end of 1848. Soon the others from the rest of US, Europe, Australia and China followed and since they mainly arrived during 1849 they were called the "forty-niners".

At first, the gold could be picked up from the ground but later on it was recovered from the streams and rivers with the use of pans. The gold rush peaked in 1852 and after that the gold reserves were getting thinner and harder to reach so that more sophisticated methods of mining had to be employed. The best results were achieved with hydraulic mining although it was environmentally damaging.

The gold rush resulted in the hasty development of California: many roads, churches, schools and towns were built to accommodate the gold-diggers. In the beginning, property rights in the goldfields were not covered by law and this was solved by the system of staking claims. The gold also helped to speed up the admission of California into the US as a State. All the preparations in terms of constitution and legislature were made in 1849 and California became a state in 1850.

Merchants v/s miners

1. California did not have the first gold rush in American history.

That honor actually belongs to North Carolina. Fifty years before gold was discovered at Sutter's mill, the first gold rush in American history got underway after a 17-pound gold nugget was found in Cabarrus County, North Carolina. Eventually, more than 30,000 people in the Tar Heel state were mining for gold, and for more than 30 years all gold coins issued by the U.S. Mint were produced using North Carolina gold.

2. The Gold Rush was the largest mass migration in U.S. history.

In March 1848, there were roughly 157,000 people in the California territory; 150,000 Native Americans, 6,500 of Spanish or Mexican descent known as Californios and fewer than 800 non-native Americans. Just 20 months later, following the massive influx of settlers, the non-native population had soared to more than 100,000. And the people just kept coming. By the mid 1850s there were more than 300,000 new arrivals—and one in every 90 people in the United

States was living in California. All of these people (and all of this money) helped fast track California to statehood. In 1850, just two years after the U.S. government had purchased the land, California became the 31st state in the Union.

3. The Gold Rush attracted immigrants from around the world.

In fact, by 1850 more than 25 percent of California's population had been born outside the United States. As news of the discovery was slow to reach the east coast, many of the first immigrants to arrive were from South America and Asia. By 1852, more than 25,000 immigrants from China alone had arrived in America. As the amount of available gold began to dwindle, miners increasingly fought one another for profits and anti-immigrant tensions soared. The government got into the action too. In 1850 California's legislature passed a Foreign Miner's tax, which levied a monthly fee of $20 on non-citizens, the equivalent of more than $500 in today's money. That bill was eventually repealed, but was replaced with another in 1852 that expressly singled out Chinese miners, charging them $2 ($80 today) a month. Violence against foreign miners increased as well, and beatings, rapes and even murders became commonplace. However no ethnic group suffered more than California's Native Americans. Before the Gold Rush, its native population numbered roughly 300,000. Within 20 years, more than 100,000 would be dead. Most died from disease or mining-related accidents, but more than 4,000 were murdered by enraged miners.

4. The Gold Rush was a male-dominated event.

Hundreds of thousands of people flocked to California to make their fortunes in the Gold Rush, but almost none of them were women. In 1852, 92 percent of the people prospecting for gold were men. The few women who did travel to the west eked out a living in the growing boomtowns, working in the restaurants, saloons and hotels that seemingly popped up every day. Some women's journals back east, fearful of the trouble the men might get into without the civilizing influence of women, published stories and ran ads encouraging educated, morally minded young women to travel west to tame these men. Few took them up on this offer. The percentage of women in gold mining communities did eventually increase somewhat, but even in 1860 they numbered fewer than 10,000—just 19 percent.

5. Early sections of San Francisco were built out of ships abandoned by prospectors.

The Gold Rush conjures up images of thousands of "'49ers" heading west in wagons to strike it rich in California, but many of the first prospectors actually arrived by ship—and few of them had a return ticket. Within months, San Francisco's port was teeming with boats that had been abandoned after their passengers—and crew—headed inland to hunt for gold. As the formerly tiny town began to boom, demand for lumber increased dramatically, and the ships were dismantled and sold as construction material. Hundreds of houses, banks, saloons, hotels, jails and other structures were built out of the abandoned ships, while others were used as landfill for lots near the waters edge. Today, more than 150 years after the Gold Rush began, archeologists and preservations continue to find relics, sometimes even entire ships, beneath the streets of the City by the Bay.

6. Prospecting for gold was a very costly enterprise.

Most of the men who flocked to northern California arrived with little more than the clothes on their backs. Once there, they needed to buy food, goods and supplies, which San Francisco's merchants were all too willing to provide—for a cost. Stuck in a remote region, far from home, many prospectors coughed up most of their hard-earned money for the most basic supplies. At the height of the boom in 1849, prospectors could expect prices sure to cause sticker shock: A single egg could cost the equivalent of $25 in today's money, coffee went for more than $100 per pound and replacing a pair of worn out boots could set you back more than $2,500.

7. More fortunes were made by merchants than by miners.

As the boom continued, more and more men got out of the gold-hunting business and began to open businesses catering to newly arrived prospectors. In fact, some of America's greatest industrialists got their start in the Gold Rush. Phillp Armour, who would later found a meatpacking empire in Chicago, made a fortune operating the sluices that controlled the flow of water into the rivers being mined. Before John Studebaker built one of America's great automobile fortunes, he manufactured wheelbarrows for Gold Rush miners. And two entrepreneurial bankers named Henry Wells and William Fargo moved west to open an office in San Francisco, an enterprise that soon grew to become one of America's premier banking institutions. One of the biggest mercantile success stories was that of Levi Strauss. A German-born tailor, Strauss arrived in San Francisco in 1850 with plans to open a store selling canvas tarps and wagon coverings to the miners. After hearing that sturdy work pants—ones that could withstand the punishing 16-hour days regularly put in by miners—were more in demand, he shifted gears, opening a store in downtown San Francisco that would eventually become a manufacturing empire, producing Levi's denim jeans.

8. Thousands of Gold Rush prospectors got rich—but John Sutter wasn't one of them.

John Sutter, the man whose land would become synonymous with the California Gold Rush, was a Swiss immigrant who fled Europe in the 1830s, leaving behind piles of unpaid debts. After several years of travelling throughout North America, he finally settled in the tiny outpost of Yuerba Buena (modern-day San Francisco) in 1839. With the assistance of the local Mexican government, Sutter quickly realized his goal of establishing an agricultural community on a 50,000-acre tract of land he called "New Helvetia," Latin for "New Switzerland, which became an important outpost for emigrants traveling to the west. It was during the construction of a sawmill on Sutter's land along the American River that one of his employees first discovered the gold nugget that would change the world. Sutter, initially more interested in maintaining control over his property, tried to keep the discovery quiet, but the news quickly leaked out. Within months, most of his workers had abandoned him to search for gold themselves, while thousands of other prospectors overran and destroyed much of his land and equipment. Faced with mounting debts, Sutter was forced to deed his land to one of his sons, who used it to create a new settlement called Sacramento. Sutter Sr. was furious—he had hoped the town would be named after him—but he had more pressing concerns. Nearly bankrupt, he began a decades-long campaign to have the U.S. government reimburse him for his financial losses, to no avail. While thousands became rich off his former land, a bitter Sutter retired to Pennsylvania and died.

South America gold

In many ways the story of Latin America, or at least the history of several countries in the region, has also been the history of mining. Spaniards found a little gold in the Caribbean but in Mexico and the Andes discovered more gold and incredibly rich silver lodes. Many of these had already been worked by the indigenous population before 1492, particularly the Andean natives, who had the most advanced pre-Columbian mining and metallurgy. During colonial times, Peru (including what would also become modern Bolivia) and Mexico were the main Spanish American mining centers, which yielded far more silver than gold. They used some slaves but primarily Indian labor to work the mines. New Granada, especially what became Colombia, was rich in gold rather than silver. The other great colonial mining region lay in Portuguese Brazil, where in the 1690s explorers found gold and three decades later diamonds. In the first quarter of the 19th century, Latin America gained its political independence, but mining remained central to life in the old mining colonies. Nonetheless, several important changes took place during the 1800s. For the first time Chile became a significant mining region, but its output consisted of copper and nitrates. Chile's comparatively stable political conditions and liberal mining policies attracted foreign investment. The older mining regions (Mexico, Peru, and Bolivia) had more difficulty adapting to independence, in part because they remained too tied to their colonial mining laws and policies but lacked the resources to subsidize the industry as Spain had done. Besides gold and silver, other minerals became important. In the early 1900s, for example, Bolivia became one of the world's leading tin producers, responding to international demand for tinned goods. Although it had another gold rush in the 1980s, Brazilian mining focused on industrial metals, such as iron (Brazil has the world's largest iron reserves). By the late 20th century, Latin Americans were also questioning the benefits of the mining industry to national development and the well-being of the populace. It seemed that mining made corporations and owners rich, at the expense of workers who often toiled for a pittance in dangerously unhealthy conditions. Cries also rose regarding the environmental damage caused by mining. Thus, Latin American mining is a subject with a long chronology and many aspects. The topic's potential bibliography is immense. What follows are some of the nuggets from that bibliography.

Mexican gold

The gold of America first came to European notice in 1492. In that year, Columbus' fleet explored the coasts of Cuba and Hispaniola and his sailors bartered Venetian glass beads, Spanish clothing, brass hawk bells and even bits of broken pottery for the golden ornaments of the natives. The West Indies were not particularly rich in precious metals but by 1530 all the major gold-producing regions of the New World from Mexico to Peru were in Spanish hands. Most of the gold jewelry was melted down on the spot but a few items were sent home as curios or as samples.

The most typical reaction in Europe was astonishment at the sheer quantity of gold flowing into Spain from the new American colonies but those connoisseurs with a more discerning eye were even more amazed by the artistic quality of the pieces.

The artist Albrecht Durer, himself the son of a goldsmith, examined part of the treasure of the Aztec

emperor Montezuma when this was displayed at court in Brussels during 1520 and wrote in his notebook ' `I saw such things which were brought to the King from the New Golden Land; a sun entirely of gold, a whole fathom broad; likewise a moon entirely of silver, just as large; likewise sundry curiosities from their weapons, arms and missiles.. . These things were all so precieus that they were valued at 100 000 guilders. But I have never in all my days seen anything that so delighted my heart as these things. For I saw amazing objects and I marvelled at the subtle ingenuity of the men in these distant lands',

Among the host of adventurers, scholars, priests and officials who came to the New World were some who had practical experience of metalworking.

Girolamo Benzoni, whose 'History of the New World' appeared in 1565, was a Milanese silversmith and jeweler, while the historian Gonzalo Fernández de Oviedo served as the king's supervisor of smelting operations in Tierra Firme (the old Spanish Main) from 1514 to 1532. Even Sir Walter Raleigh, in his abortive search for the legendary `Golden Citie of Manoa', collected important information about the melting and casting of gold alloys in Guyana (1).

By combining these early eyewitness accounts with modern laboratory analyses of museum specimens, it is possible to build up a fairly detailed picture of aboriginal gold technology as it was at the moment of European contact.

One of the best sixteenth century accounts of Indian metalsmiths at work comes from Garcilaso de la Vega, son of a Spanish father and an Inca mother. Describing the processes of melting and hammering in the Andes before the adoption of European technology, he commented:

They never make anvils of iron or any other metal. .. They used hard stones of a colour between green and yellow as anvils.

They planed and smoothed them against one another, and esteemed them highly, since they were very rare. They could not make hammers with wooden handles. They worked with instruments of copper and brass mixed together, and shaped like dice with rounded corners. Some are as large as the hand can grasp for heavy work; others are medium sized, others small, and others elongated for hammering a concave shape.

They hold these hammers in the hand and strike with them like cobblestones. They had no files or graving tools, nor bellows for founding. Their founding they did by blowing down copper pipes, according to the size of the work. These pipes were blocked at one end, but had a small hole through which the air came out compressed and with greater force. It might be necessary to use eight, ten or twelve at once according to the furnace. They walked round the fire blowing. . Nor had they tongs for getting the metal out of the fire',

Although Garcilaso was writing specifically about Andean silversmiths, the technology he describes was widespread in South and Central America.

African gold

Eastern and Southern Africa, 1000–1400 A.D.

Eastern and Southern Africa, 1400–1600 A.D.

Guinea Coast, 1400–1600 A.D.

Western and Central Sudan, 1000–1400 A.D.

Western and Central Sudan, 1400–1600 A.D.

Western North Africa (The Maghrib), 500–1000 A.D.

Western North Africa (The Maghrib), 1000–1400 A.D.

Western North Africa (The Maghrib), 1400–1600 A.D.

Western Sudan, 500–1000 A.D.

The Mineral Wealth of Africa

The continent of Africa is the location of the birth of humankind. It has forever been the cradle of life for all of humankind's needs, wants, and desires. Within the earth is a veritable treasure trove; wonders of beauty and stores of energy that have long since propelled people to greatness with the acquisition of their bounty.

Gold was first used industrially in Egypt around 3100 BCE. It was mined from the granite filled mountains that are found in the eastern part of the country as well as in what once was called Nubia. Slave labor was used to mine for the gold because so much of it was required for the worship of the god Ra, to build temples, and for personal adornment.

Gold in West Africa

In West Africa, an ancient people called the Akan populated the location that we now call Ghana around the 11th-century CE. Among the many tribes of this ancient civilization, could be found, the ethnic groups of the Ashanti and the Fanti, who mined for gold along the rivers Volta and Ankobra. The Akan divided gold collection based on sex.

Akan women were responsible for panning for gold along the rivers. After a heavy rainfall, women could find gold littered along the riverbed that could be easily obtained by hand. These pieces of gold were mainly small nuggets. Women could easily see these nuggets after the rainy seasons of the spring and would use wooden bowls to dig in the sand along the shore.

Afterward, they would shake the bowls, allowing the sand and gold to sink to the bottom. They would pour out the water and pick the gold from what remained. This process continued by transferring the remaining sand and dirt to smaller bowls with water, and shaking until all of the gold had been picked from the sand that had been collected initially.

Akan men were responsible for mining for gold, which was much more dangerous and painstaking. Mines within the earth were notorious for collapsing after the heavy spring rains, and many Akan men lost their lives. Men dug 60-foot holes into the ground with iron tools, then, as a team, they transported wooden bowls from deep within the mines, filled with dirt and gold to the top.

Gold Akan Artifact

Golden Akan Artifact

This gold was then traded for salt and slaves with the Berber tribes of northern Africa. The Akan needed salt for food preservation, and the Berbers used the gold and salt for currency and trade with the Arab world, of the Middle East. By the 1400s, the Portuguese arrived in western Africa and began trading gold with the

Akan again for slaves and other things like brass. The Portuguese found so much gold along the rivers of western Africa that soon other Europeans would be attracted to the area.

By the 1600's the Portuguese had been replaced by the Dutch who later joined by the British in 1651. The two vied for dominance over tribes like the Akan in order to control the gold trade in West Africa which was also thriving on the slave trade. The British would emerge victoriously and would control the area known as the Gold Coast until 1957 when the area became known as Ghana.

Throne of Ashanti Rulers-Golden Stool

Gold in South Africa

Between the 10th and 13th centuries CE, the South African kingdom of Mapungubwe thrived due to natural resources like gold. Located in the areas of modern-day Zimbabwe, Botswana, and South Africa, Mapungubwe did mu

Gold Trade and the Kingdom of Ancient Ghana

Around the fifth century, thanks to the availability of the camel, Berber-speaking people began crossing the Sahara Desert. From the eighth century onward, annual trade caravans followed routes later described by Arabic authors with minute attention to detail. Gold, sought from the western and central Sudan, was the main commodity of the trans-Saharan trade. The traffic in gold was spurred by the demand for and supply of coinage. The rise of the Soninke empire of Ghana appears to be related to the beginnings of the trans-Saharan gold trade in the fifth century.

From the seventh to the eleventh century, trans-Saharan trade linked the Mediterranean economies that demanded gold—and could supply salt—to the sub-Saharan economies, where gold was abundant. Although local supply of salt was sufficient in sub-Saharan Africa, the consumption of Saharan salt was promoted for trade purposes. In the eighth and ninth centuries, Arab merchants operating in southern Moroccan towns such as Sijilmasa bought gold from the Berbers, and financed more caravans. These commercial transactions encouraged further conversion of the Berbers to Islam. Increased demand for gold in the North Islamic states, which sought the raw metal for minting, prompted scholarly attention to Mali and Ghana, the latter referred to as the "Land of Gold." For instance, geographer al-Bakri described the eleventh-century court at Kumbi Saleh, where he saw gold-embroidered caps, golden saddles, shields and swords mounted with gold, and dogs' collars adorned with gold and silver. The Soninke managed to keep the source of their gold (the Bambuk mines, most notably) secret from Muslim traders. Yet gold production and trade were important activities that undoubtedly mobilized hundreds of thousands of African people. Leaders of the ancient kingdom of Ghana accumulated wealth by keeping the core of pure metal, leaving the unworked native gold to be marketed by their people.

Gold Trade and the Mali Empire

By 1050, Ghana was strong enough to assume control of the Islamic Berber town of Audaghost. By the end of the twelfth century, however, Ghana had lost its domination of the western Sudan gold trade. Trans-Saharan routes began to bypass Audaghost, expanding instead toward the newly opened Bure goldfield. Soso, the southern chiefdom of the Soninke, gained control of Ghana as well as the Malinke, the latter eventually liberated by Sundiata Keita, who founded the Mali empire. Mali rulers did not encourage gold producers to convert to Islam, since prospecting and production of the metal traditionally depended on a number of beliefs and magical practices that were alien to Islam. In the fourteenth century, cowrie shells were introduced from the eastern coast as local currency, but gold and salt remained the principal mediums of long-distance trade.

The flow of sub-Saharan gold to the northeast probably occurred in a steady but small stream. Mansa Musa's arrival in Cairo carrying a ton of the metal (1324–25) caused the market in gold to crash, suggesting that the average supply was not as great. Undoubtedly, some of this African gold was also used in Western gold coins. African gold was indeed so famous worldwide that a Spanish map of 1375 represents the king of Mali holding a gold nugget (Bibliothèque Nationale de France, Paris). When Mossi raids destroyed the Mali empire, the rising Songhai empire relied on the same resources. Gold remained the principal product in the trans-Saharan trade, followed by kola nuts and slaves. The Moroccan scholar Leo Africanus, who visited Songhai in 1510 and 1513, observed that the governor of Timbuktu owned many articles of gold, and that the coin of Timbuktu was made of gold without any stamp or superscription.

Citation. Department of the Arts of Africa, Oceania, and the Americas. "The Trans-Saharan Gold Trade (7th–14th Century Century)." In Heilbrunn Timeline of Art History. New York: The Metropolitan Museum of Art, 2000–.
http://www.metmuseum.org/toah/hd/gold/hd_gold.html

Egyptologists have long noted that the surfaces of many ancient Egyptian objects made of gold bear a distinctive coloration that ranges from a pale reddish hue to a dark purple. This effect is observed on solid cast figures as well as on hammered sheet metal and gold leaf, such that its origin would seem to be independent of the technology used for fabrication. A typical example is the gilded face mask on the mummy of Ukhhotep (12.182.132). While the effect has been recognized for more than a century, its cause remained a subject of speculation until recently. Over the years, numerous hypotheses have been advanced to explain the phenomenon, including tarnishing of a debased gold alloy, remanent colloidal gold following selective corrosion and removal of alloying elements such as silver and copper, deposition of organic films, and adventitious or deliberate addition of iron-bearing minerals such as hematite or pyrite to the gold alloy. Notably, Alfred Lucas, one of the foremost early researchers in the study of ancient Egyptian technology, correctly surmised that the vast majority of such colorations resulted from fortuitous tarnishing of silver-bearing gold and also recognized correctly that a smaller group of objects bearing a distinctly different red coloration represented another phenomenon altogether.

The idea that this coloration derives from a corrosion process and not a deliberate patination is prompted partly by the fact that nearly all native gold occurs as an alloy of gold and silver known as electrum, and partly by occurrences of the coloration in what are sometimes observed to be seemingly irregular distributions on the surfaces of objects. The most notable examples of this kind are the gold-leaf decorations on the wood sarcophagus enclosures from the tomb of Tutankhamun, where areas of bright gold leaf are seen juxtaposed against areas of a dark purple coloration along irregular borders that would seem to have no relationship to an intended design.

Early attempts to analyze the red colorations often were confounded by the extremely small thicknesses of the layers, such that samples obtained by scraping—no matter how judiciously performed—were usually overwhelmed by contamination from the substrate alloy. However, analysis in situ by x-ray diffractometry and x-ray fluorescence spectrometry has provided a rapid and straightforward way of characterizing the films and has shown them typically to be composed of one or more silver-gold sulfides. The species responsible for the predominant reddish purple coloration is most often indicated to be $AgAuS$, a compound sometimes found in nature as the mineral petrovskaite. In addition, synthetic gold-silver alloys having a silver content between approximately 8 and 11 weight percent silver have been observed to develop red-purple tarnish films identical in appearance and composition to those found on ancient Egyptian silver-gold objects when exposed to sulfide ion for extended periods at elevated temperatures. With increasing silver content and prolonged exposure to sulfide ion, both historical gold-silver objects and modern synthetic gold-silver surfaces develop black tarnishes that include another phase, Ag_3AuS_2, which also occurs in nature as the mineral uytenbogaardtite. Taken together, the evidence suggests that the red colorations derive largely—as Lucas first conjectured—from fortuitous tarnishing of native electrum having silver-gold compositions appropriate for the formation of the $AgAuS$ phase.

Red sulfide tarnishes have been identified on historical gold-silver objects from other cultural contexts, including goldwork from the Royal Cemetery at Ur

(33.35.3) and nineteenth-century European jewelry. That these tarnishes occur predominantly on ancient Egyptian objects likely reflects the high sulfide ion activity associated with the typical contexts of sealed burial chambers as well as the unparted gold-silver alloys used in antiquity.

As a footnote to the discussion, it should be added that not all red-purple colorations on historical gold objects belong to the sulfide-tarnish group described here. Indeed, as Lucas also observed, a small number of gold pieces from the tomb of Tutankhamun bear a bright, translucent red coloration on their surfaces distinctly different in appearance from the darker and more opaque examples. The origin of the color on these unusual objects has not been determined, but may well reside in the deliberate or accidental addition of iron-bearing compounds to the gold, as synthetic samples of such composition have yielded similar appearing surfaces. There also occur archaeological gold objects that bear reddish accretions of hydrated iron oxides, such as lepidocrocite, presumably deposited as residues from groundwater during burial, as well as the gold masks and other objects from Precolumbian South America that exhibit deliberately applied coatings of the red mercuric sulfide mineral cinnabar (1974.271.35). Finally, we should mention that the addition of copper to gold in several types of Egyptian objects during the reign of Akhenaten appears to have been done for its rutilizing effect, and that during the Third Intermediate Period copper-rich gold inlays were used with precious-metal inlays of other compositions and hues for the embellishment of large figural bronzes.

China gold

As the largest producer of gold in the world, China's gold reserves are spread across a number of orogenic belts that were constructed around ancient craton margins during various subduction–collision cycles, as well as within the cratonic interior along reactivated paleo-sutures. Among the major gold deposits in China is the unique class of world's richest gold mines in the Jiaodong Peninsula in the eastern part of the North China Craton with an overall endowment of > 3000 tons. Following the dawn of metal in the third millennium BC in western China, placer gold mining was soon in practice, particularly during the Xia, Shang and Zhou dynasties. During 1096 AD, mining techniques were developed to dig underground tunnels and the earliest mineral processing technology was in place to pan gold from crushed rock ores. However, ancient China did not witness any major breakthrough in gold exploitation and production, and the growth in the gold ownership was partly due to the 'Silk Road' that enabled the sale of silk products and exquisite artifacts to the west in exchange of gold products. In the modern times, the proven reserves of gold resources in China have steadily increased from 4614.7 tons in 2005 up to 6864.79 tons in 2010, with a growth rate of 48.76%. In the past ten years, the rate of production increased by 70%, launching China as the top producer of gold in the world in 2008 when the production reached 300 tons per year. The gross industrial output of gold industry in China increased sharply from 20.82 billion Yuan up to 229.29 billion Yuan between 2000 and 2010, registering 9 times growth, and breaking the world record. A simultaneous hike in the proportion of gross value in GDP from 0.21% in 2003 up to 0.58% in 2010 is also recorded.

RuiZhangHuayanPianM.SantoshShoutingZhang

School of Earth Sciences and Resources, China University of Geosciences Beijing, 29 Xueyuan Road, Beijing 100083, China

Ancient Israel

In the wake of successive conquests, Ancient Palestine was subjected to a variety of cultural influences. Gold objects found in excavations there reflect these influences and bear witness to the importance of the area as a main trade route.

With centres of civilisation to both its east and its west, and as a natural passageway between these centres, Ancient Palestine was conquered repeatedly by invaders who left imprints on the land not only of their various beliefs and customs, but also of those of their trading partners. The gold artefacts which have been found in excavations in Ancient Palestine are therefore of particular interest in relation to the historica) periods during which they were made.

Gold in the Canaanite Period

Although archaeological excavations along the coastal strip of Israel have unearthed graves furnished

with pottery, weapons and very simple jewellery, only a few Early Canaanite gold artefacts have been

discovered (1,2), Thus, several simple round gold beads made from gold leaf and found in Azor, near

Jaffa, are the earliest specimens of gold in this area.

They date back to between 3200 and 2850 B.C. In addition, a small disc in repoussé technique has

been found, along with gold beads, in a tomb in Beth Yerah near the Sea of Galilee. It dates back to

between 2850 and 2650 B.C. and is decorated by punching with dotted circles and lines extending from

the centre like the arms of a cross. The technique and motif have parallels among contemporary gold pendants from graves in Anatolia but there is no indication of whether the disc was an imitation produced by a local craftsman or an import.

There is archaeological evidence also, that gold was available for widespread jewellery production in Canaan from the second part of the Middle Bronze Age (1800 to 1500 B.C.), the period of the Hyksos domination of Canaan, until the Late Bronze Age (1500 to 1200 B.C.). The renewed Egyptian rule with the rise of the XVIIIth Dynasty (1580 B.C.) brought a prosperous period to the Canaanite city states, which sheltered the sanctuaries of their own gods side by side with those of the Egyptians (3,4).

At the time, the main sources of gold were Egypt and Arabia.

The two significant sources of Egyptian gold was found in a place called Nubia toward the South and in the Eastern deserts. Much of this is now part of present-day Sudan.

So far there have been over a hundred ancient gold workings and settlements that have been discovered in Egypt, the vast majority of them in the dry Eastern Desert. According to the map on the Turin Papyrus, there were no less than 1300 such mines in the ancient Egypt.

Already quite a number of old mines have been discovered in several other places throughout the Nubian and the eastern deserts pointing to the existence of more such ancient times gold mine

Most of the mines in Ancient Egypt were state monopolies and were worked dominatingly by prisoners and slaves. According to the syntheses of the understudy of history, Diodorus Siculus in his Bibliotheca Historica published around 60 BCE, these miners were made to work in astonishingly difficult conditions, with little food or water and were often beaten if they didn't work hard enough.

However, many archaeologists now believe that much of the gold was actually acquired through barter with people called the Kushites, a civilization that ruled south of the Egyptians.

There have been thousands of mining sites in this region, indicating that a considerable amount of gold was being mined and traded.

The Persian, Greek, Roman and Byzantine Periods

Relatively little jewellery has been found from the periods in which Palestine was successively a part of

the Persian, Greek, Roman and Byzantine empires, as compared with the amounts found in Canaanite hoards. The objects discovered well reflect the characteristic features of their period and their style is strongly reminiscent of that of the dominant civilization of the time. The fact that no moulds have been found, however, raises doubts as to whether gold artefacts were actually produced locally.

A Persian gold Barring from the fourth century B.C. has recently been found in Ashdod, which depicts a wild goat in the Achaemenid style. Such earrings were common in Persia and many parts of the Persian Empire and moulds for similar objects have been discovered in Egypt and in Byblos.

A pair of earrings from the Roman period (second or third century A.D.), in the shape of a basket entirely made in delicate filigree work, has been found in Hamat Tiberias.

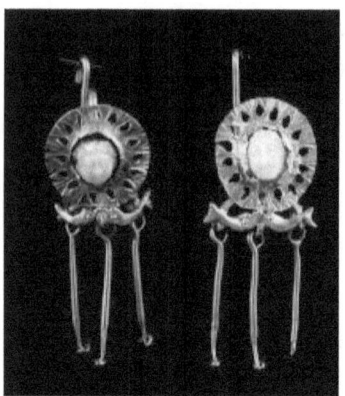

The Hellenistic influence is pronounced in this specimen. A gold diadem found in a tomb in Kfar Giladi and a pair of earrings from Jerusalem illustrate polychrome and fretwork techniques.

A coloured semi-precious stone is the main decorative element, whereas the gold frame is of simple

repoussé work.

 Small magical gold plaques from a tomb in Jaffa, used during the process of mummification,

were also executed in simple repoussé technique, having incised lines as the main decorative element.

Jewellery decorated with Christian themes appeared in Palestine in the Byzantine period (sixth century A.D.). One of the best examples was found in the excavations at the Temple Mount. It is a gold ring to which is attached a decorative structure which probably represents the grave of Jesus Christ.

Nabataean Jewellery

The Nabataeans were Arabic tribes who had settled in Transjordania and the central Negev at the end of

the fourth century B.C. They lived there, though discontinuously, for 500 years. Their successive periods of rise and fall were associated with the periods of stabilization and decline of the Hellenic, Roman and Byzantine empires. They were mainly occupied with the caravan trade through the stretches of desert between Syria and Arabia, transporting goods from the Mediterranean to the Red Sea, and they succeeded in transforming the road stops in the desert into flourishing cities in which Arabian gold concentrated.

Some of the Nabataean cemetries have remained undisturbed by grave-robbers and most of the tombs until the middle of the third century contain gold jewellery. According to the Greek religious custom adopted by the Nabataeans, the men were buried with a coin in the mouth or with a pendant, so that they would have payment ready for Charon for the crossing of the River Styx at the entrance to the

Underworld. The women were buried with two pairs of earrings. Those of one pair were small and made of thin gold sheet fabricated into tubular boat shapes.

Such earrings were known in the Near East from the second millennium B.C. These simple earrings were possibly given to the women in their youth.

Gold in the Islamic Culture of Palestine From the seventh century A.D. onwards, the Islamic cultural element was added to those of the many peoples who lived in Palestine. An example of the use of gold in the Early Islamic period is illustrated by mosaics in the Dome of the Rock (the Mosque of Omar), built by Abd-al-Malik at the end of the seventh century . There are beautifully rendered fruit-bearing trees, palmettes, candelabra and acanthus scrolls — inspired by a hybrid of Hellenistic, Roman and Sassanian sources. The tesserae forming the gold background, vary in size from 0.25 to 1 cm 2 . They are set in plaster, forming regular horizontal courses one above the other.

Each is fixed with its axis not at right angles to the surface of the wall but at an angle of about 30 degrees.

The golden surface is thus not smooth, for each course of tesserae has a sloping face, with several courses together making a zig-zag line. The tesserae have fallen in many places and imitations in paint.

have been made over the years, but fragments of the original mosaic have survived on one of the jambs of the eastern window of the drum and on the outer walls of the shrine.

Few Islamic gold jewellery pieces have been found which date from this period. However, recently a beautiful necklace of granulation and filigree work from the Late Islamic period (early eleventh century) was discovered in a jar hidden in the Arabic occupation layer in Caesarea. The necklace consists of six large round beads of sheet gold ornamented by granulation, together with round and biconical beads in very fine filigree work. The large beads are linked together with three rows of small heads, some are made of sheet gold and others in filigree. The quality of the piece is an indication of the high degree of skill attained by the Islamic goldsmiths.

Phoenician Goldware

The Phoenicians as a people cannot be differentiated from the general mass of Canaanites until the later half of the second millennium B.C. They lived in the northern part of Palestine and on the coastal strip of Lebanon. A brief description of Phoenician gold craft is worth including here because it had a definite and direct influence on developments in neighboring Palestine, mainly during the Israeli period.

As the natural resources of their country were meagre, the Phoenicians developed maritime trade at an early date and maintained close commercial relations with the Minoans and Mycenaeans in the west and with the Assyrians in the east. Thanks to these contacts, they became innovators in metal work, especially in precious metals.

Their gold was obtained from Ethiopia, Arabia and Asia Minor. Remains of smelters have not been found

but harmers, tongs and other metal-working tools are depicted on funerary stelae.

Longer Time Frame for African History

Slavery and African slaves have dominated historical perspectives of Africa and its relations with the wider world. Yet, it is gold which has been the most important and enduring element that has shaped and determined West Africa and its interactions with the wider world. For at least 1,500 years gold and not slaves has been the commodity determining not only the region's economy and history, but also West Africa's links with the wider world.

Beginning in the late 1700s, understandable humanitarian concerns and philanthropic motives ensured that the focal point within public discussion and history, when dealing with West Africa, came to be centered on the issue of slavery. Focusing on slavery to the detriment of gold and other commodities to some extent ensured that the export of slaves from West Africa came to be halted in the course of the nineteenth century. The persistence of slavery within Africa, as well as the continued smuggling of slaves out of Africa, in many instances served to legitimate the intervention in, and subsequent occupation of, West Africa by Europe's imperial powers. Ironically, those opposed to colonial rule made grateful use of the historical trope of slavery that existed within European discourse to hasten the end of colonial occupation in West Africa. Thus the discourse that had in many instances been used to legitimate the establishment of colonial rule, was also used to oppose colonial rule. But, and this is the important issue, in both instances it was the trope of 'slavery' that determined the manner in which lay and professional observers looked at West Africa's past. In both instances it was a dehumanizing and debilitating view of history that effectively robbed, and continues to rob, West African historical actors of any agency beyond being mere pawns in the West's insatiable thirst and desire for slaves. The persistence of this negative history continues to rob West Africa of its rightful place in global history.

The focus on slavery has overshadowed and driven from both public and scholarly perception the realization that West Africa's history is far more than slavery alone; it is indeed a sad irony of history that the incessant focus on the dark past of slavery has managed to eclipse the bright history of gold in West Africa. A refocus of West African history, away from the past three hundred years to the longer perspective of nearly two thousand years, brings into focus a far more constructive and less passive history of West Africa and its inhabitants. Far from being merely the subject pawns of the deeply exploitative and dehumanizing trade and economic systems initiated outside of Africa, a refocus on the role of West African gold in its relations with the wider world, brings to the fore a far more energetic and virile history in which West Africa's relations with the rest of the world are based on a far greater degree of equality and shared interest.

This essay has been written with the express purpose of drawing to the fore the long history of gold in West Africa so that a new beginning can be made to refocus views of Africa and its people away from a debilitating and ultimately nihilistic focus on slavery. A focus on the long-term history West African gold will bring to the fore an interesting history in which Africans are not merely acted upon but ultimately determined the course of global history and humanity.

There are three principal points, all of which relate to the period prior to 1900. These three points are:

– Gold is widespread and accessible across West Africa. That gold is to be found across West Africa in such a manner that people can access it without resorting to forms of technology other than those that they would normally use in their existence as non-mechanized agriculturalists;

– Between 400 and 1500 West Africa was the world's most important supplier of gold;

– The central role of Mande speaking peoples and Mande forms of social structure in coming to an understanding of the exploitation of gold in West Africa.

Broadly speaking, apart from the three points listed above, from approximately 1000 BC to 1800 AD, and roughly geographically from North, on the northern fringes of the Sahara, to South-West to the southern fringes of the Sahara, before ending in the South-East in the forest zones of West Africa and the shore of the Atlantic Ocean. Travelling through time and space we will touch upon the people referred to as the Garamantes in the Libyan desert, the ancient states of Ghana and Mali in what is today the Sahel of West Africa, before concluding with the Akan/Ashante forest polities in present-day Ghana.

Agriculturalists' Gold

The gradual desiccation of the Sahara that began approximately 5,000 years ago served to concentrate human populations on the fringes of the desert. South of the Sahara agricultural communities came to be established around 1000 BC. For the past two thousand years members of these agricultural communities on the southern fringes of the Sahel have resorted to gold production for part of the year. Throughout the region 'placer' deposits have been prospected and mined for gold by agriculturalists during periods of the year in which the agricultural cycle came to a standstill.

Throughout West Africa gold mining has concentrated on placer deposits across a very large area with comparatively little reef mining. The mining of placer deposits has been possible with little technological investment, and was well within the reach of agricultural communities living in the areas concerned. As in the present, agriculturalists sought to supplement their income through searching for gold.

Instead, countless small gold workings across an extensive area of West Africa obscured the existence of a single well defined mine which people outside the area believed existed in the area. Instead, people outside of the area, who were ignorant of the extent of the extensive series of small-scale agriculturalist gold workings, believed that the alleged single source of the gold was being consciously hidden from them by the West African kingdoms that developed in the area. It was precisely because placer deposits were so widely spread, and were so accessible to agriculturalists, that West Africa was able to produce gold so very much.

Garamantes

The Garamantes were Berber semi-pastoralists who lived almost directly south of what would become Carthage and controlled the trade going into and coming out of the Sahara from West Africa. The Garamantes are believed to have adopted horse-drawn chariots from Egypt in the late second millennium BC and riding horses in the first millennium BC (Iliffe 1995: 30). Rock art in the Sahara indicates that regular lines of communication were open to the Sudanic belt from the Mediterranean via the Garamantes as early as 500 BC. The drawings, mainly of chariots or carts, some horse drawn, and some bullock drawn, have allowed some to tentatively re-construct the trade routes that might have existed across the desert, and even to differentiate between routes.

Trade to and from West Africa was possible via wagon routes, yet with the ever further desiccation the Sahara became ever more of a boundary, eventually the Sahara became insurmountable for donkeys, horses and bullocks. Yet while it lasted the Garamantes controlled and determined the trade across the desert. Somewhat fancifully, Herodotus (n.d.) noted of the Garamantes:

Ten days' journey from Augila there is again a salt-hill and a spring; palms of the fruitful kind grow here abundantly, as they do also at the other salt-hills. This region is inhabited by a nation called the Garamantians, a very powerful people, who cover the salt with mould, and then sow their crops. From thence is the shortest road to the Lutophagi, a journey of thirty days. In the Garamantian country are found the oxen which, as they graze, walk backwards. This they do because their horns curve outwards in front of their heads, so that it is not possible for them when grazing to move forwards, since in that case their horns would become fixed in the ground. Only herein do they differ from other oxen, and further in the thickness and hardness of their hides. The Garamantians have four-horse chariots, in which they chase the Troglodyte Ethiopians, who of all the nations whereof any account has reached our ears are by far the swiftest of foot. The Troglodytes feed on serpents, lizards, and other similar reptiles. Their language is unlike that of any other people; it sounds like the screeching of bats.

It has been suggested that the Garamantians traded directly with the Bambuk around the headwaters of the Senegal and Niger rivers, yet this is highly unlikely. None the less, the Phoenician settlement of Carthage, established due north of the Garamantians on the Mediterranean coast was fabled for its gold, which may very well have come from West Africa via Garamantes.

It is probable that by the time of the destruction of Carthage in 146 BC trade across the Sahara had come to a standstill. It would be at least another five hundred years before any form of regular trade came to be established across the Sahara again. Not until the camel had been introduced from Arabia into North Africa by the Romans in around 100 AD would it be possible for people to regularly and reliably traverse the Sahara. From at least 400 AD onwards camel mounted Berber established trade routes across the Sahara to West Africa. The camel and the caravans it enabled came to dominate the trans-Saharan trade until the second half of the twentieth century.

The introduction of the camel allowed for constant communication to be maintained between the Berbers on both shores of the Sahara. With their camels these people, bridged the desert, and carried an ever-growing trade, in whichouthbound salt was exchanged for northbound gold. There were four principal routes across the Sahara:

– The Salima trail from Cyrenacia to Wadai;

– The Bilma Trail or Garamantes road from Tripoli to Kawar;

– The Gadames Road from Ghat to the Hausa country;

– The Sijilmassa – Walata Road from Morocco to the Middle Niger and Upper Senegal.

Each of these routes represented a two month journey, with long waterless stretches between oases. The most important of these routes, Sijilmasa to Walata, was founded on the gold of the Upper Niger that was exchanged for the salt of the Saharan oases of Tagaza and Taodeni.

It has to be borne in mind that when, following the introduction of the camel, the trans-Saharan trade routes were explored and established, the first Berber traders to reach the southern shores of the Sahel found an already long-established and extensive trading system within West Africa. That is, the trans-Saharan trade and outside influence did not initiate the initial establishment of West African trading systems or political units; instead the Berber allowed for the intermeshing of two previously wholly separate trading systems, that of the Mediterranean and that of West Africa. As Iliffe succinctly noted (1995: 81): 'The chief reason why trans-Saharan trade grew so swiftly in the early Islamic period was probably that it linked two flourishing regional economies.'

For its part West Africa contributed gold to the new trading linkages and for the coming 1,100 years, until the European discovery of America, West Africa supplied the bulk of the known world's gold.

Sudanese States: Ghana and Mali

From around 400 AD a series of Sudanese states rose to ascendancy and eventual decline. Amongst the most well-known of these states are Ghana and Mali. Although historians refer to these states as kingdoms or empires, it has to be borne in mind that they have taken terms and concepts drawn from European history and transferred them onto an African reality which culturally and politically was different to Europe (see, for instance, Jansen 1996).

The medieval state of Ghana (not to be confused with present-day republic of Ghana) was established by Mande speaking people in the Hawd region around Kumbi Saleh in present-day southern Mauretania. It is remembered by the present-day Soninke as the state of Wagadu. Medieval Ghana's population developed iron working techniques and established a centre of authority which traded across the Sahara. Gold was mined to the south of the newly emergent polity at the headwaters of Niger and Senegal rivers in what has become known as the Bure and Bambuk goldfields respectively.

Traders and merchants from Ghana traded for gold from these mining areas by means of what has become known as 'silent trade', or dumb barter. Upon reaching the gold mining regions the Ghanaian traders would place their trade goods on the ground, then they would beat on large drums and blow on trumpets, before withdrawing out of sight. The local Africans would then emerge and place what they believed to be the equivalent value in gold on the ground next to the goods they wished to trade for. The Africans would then withdraw, and the traders would re-emerge. If the traders agreed with the exchange rate being offered, they would take the gold and once again beat their drums and blow their trumpets before withdrawing with the trade being completed. The gold would then be taken to the market towns of Kumbi Saleh or Aoudaghost, the southern terminus of the western trans-Sahara trade route that led from Marrekesh in Morocco. In these towns the gold would be exchanged for salt and exotic Mediterranean goods transported across the Sahara by North African merchants. Through controlling the trade and taxing the import and export of goods transported to Ghana in exchange for gold the Ghanaian state was able to accrue wealth and strengthen its position.

As the west African Sudan and Sahel is largely bereft of salt, and salt was in short supply everywhere in the region, it 'was literally worth its weight in gold' to Africans in West Africa at the time (Crowder 1977: 28). The oases town of Taghaza, which was built completely from salt and was entirely dependent on food transported into the town from the North and the South depended solely on its production of salt.

When the Arabs conquered North Africa in the seventh century, they discovered that Berber nomads on camels had long established trade links with Ghana, and that the main item of trade was gold. This was of importance to the Arabs for their monetary system was based on gold. For the coming eight hundred years, until the Americas were brought into direct contact with Europe and Asia, West Africa was to become the prime source of gold in Europe and the Levant. By the eighth century Ghana's fame as 'the land of Gold' had reached the court of the Caliph in Baghdad, where news of its existence was recorded by the geographer Al-Fazari (Crowder 1977: 27). According to the early tenth-century geographer Ibn al-Faqih, gold grew there 'in the sand, as carrots do, and is picked at sunrise' (in Wright 2007: 19).

The Arab conquest of North Africa gave the trans-Saharan trade a new impetus by linking it with a vast empire, anxious to obtain as much as possible of its gold, on which the monetary system of the muslim world depended. Traders from the eastern parts of the Muslim world, mainly from Iraq, were attracted to towns at the northern end of the trans-Saharan trails.

The Andalusian Spanish Arab traveler Abu Ubayd Al-Bakri visited the court of Tunku Menin, the reigning ruler of Ghana in the year 1065. Upon his return to Andalusia Al-Bakri wrote The Book of Routes and Kingdoms and noted that Ghana's ruler commanded an army of no less than 200,000 men, of whom 40,000 were bowmen. He levied taxes on imported salt and gold, thus for every donkey load of sold transported into Ghana he levied a tax of one dinar in gold. His subjects were permitted to sell gold dust, but all nuggets were the property of the ruler and remained under his control (Crowder 1977: 30). Al-Bakri (cited in Iliffe 1995: 51) wrote of the ruler of Ghana:

The king has a palace and a number of domed dwellings all surrounded with an enclosure like a city wall (...) The king adorns himself like a woman (with gold) round his neck and on his forearms, and he puts on a high cap decorated with gold and wrapped in a turban of fine cotton. He sits in audience or to hear grievances against officials in a domed pavilion around which stand ten horses covered with gold-embroidered materials. Behind the king stand ten pages holding shields and swords decorated with gold, and on his right are the sons of the (subject) kings of his country wearing splendid garments and their hair plaited with gold.

The ruler of Ghana never fully embraced Islam but maintained good relations with Islamic traders from North Africa. The capital of Ghana, probably Kumbi Saleh, in Southern Mauritania was divided into two cities, one Islamic with twelve mosques and six miles away the royal capital with its own mosque but also the stronghold of traditional religion. The rise of the Almoravids, who would later occupy Spain, brought about an end to the traditional religion of Ghana and ended its dominance.

Across West Africa, the Soninke recall the collapse of Ghana with a legend about 'Wagadu' that brings to the fore the conflict that existed in medieval Ghana between Islam and the traditional religion of its leaders. A traditional religion that ensured the fertility of the goldfields upon which the state depended. Crowder & Ajayi summarize the legend as follows (1971: 125):

Wagadu was blessed with vast amounts of gold, replenished annually, thanks to the guardian of the kingdom, a snake. The snake was worshipped in an annual sacrifice of a virgin. Catastrophe came about when the lover of the virgin chosen to be sacrificed killed the snake. The dying snake pronounced a dreadful curse, causing the desiccation of the land and the cessation of the gold, which moved to Bure on the Upper Niger. As a result the people dispersed and their country turned into desert.

Elizabeth Isichei (1997: 224) wrote of this tradition: 'It is an extraordinarily vivid symbolic representation of the decline of a kingdom, the advent of Islam, and the degeneration of the enivironment.'

Ghana came to be established in the fourth century, essentially at that moment in time when North African Berber traders were able to effectively use the camel to cross the Sahara. Ghana developed its position through being positioned in such a way that it could control the flow of gold from both the Bure and Bambuk goldfields as it moved northwards to the terminus on the southern shore of the Sahara desert. Perfectly positioned to control the trade Ghana existed for approximately eight hundred years until it collapsed in the early 1200s.

Undoubtedly the most remarkable and well known history in West Africa is that of Sunjata, the 'Lion King' (jata = 'lion'; 'Sun' is from Sogolon, his mother's name), and the society he founded, called 'Mali' or 'Mande'. All across the Sahel griots and hunters' bards continue to recount the trials and tribulations of Sunjata. Indeed, it has been argued that the political system that came about on account of Sunjata's activities continues to influence and determine social structure within Mande societies across West Africa (cf. Jansen 1996).

Mansa Musa

The epic of Sunjata notes that the history of Mali begins with Sunjata's defeat of the oppressive Soso blacksmith-king Sumaoro Kanté. Shortly there after Sunjata claimed and gained the allegiance of people from the headwaters of the Niger to the Sahara in the North and the Senegal in the West. Essentially the economy of Mali was based on the agriculture of its people, supplemented by profits gained from control and taxation of the trade in gold. Taxation was invested into an army of chain-mailed cavalry that extended the empire to the Atlantic. The early fourteenth century became the golden age of Mali; the empire came most spectacularly to the attention of the world during the reign of Mansa Musa (1312-1337) the most famous of the Mali rulers. It was Mansa Musa's pilgrimage to Mecca in 1324 that literally put Mali on the map. During his stay in Egypt on his way to Mecca he spent and gave away so much gold that there was a major devaluation of currency. The Catalan map of Abraham Cresques shows Mussa Melli seated on a golden throne, wearing a golden crown, and describes him as 'the richest and most noble king in all the land' (quoted in Crowder 1977: 32).

Ibn Battuta

Shortly after the reign of Mansa Musa, the Arabic traveller Ibn Battuta, travelled to Mali in 1352. He provided first hand descriptions of the ruler of Mali as sitting on cushions of the finest silks, bedecked with expensive European cloth, with a golden crown and a parasol topped with a golden bird the size of a falcon, and being praised by a group of musicians as the most venerable descendant and successor of Sunjata (Ibn Battuta 1929: 326). Ibn Battuta's detailed reports provide also a first-hand account of the journey from the Mediterranean across the Sahara via the oasis Sijilmasa to Taghaza, the first town within the jurisdiction of the ruler of Mali. Not surprisingly, Ibn Battuta disliked Taghaza, a hot, smelly, fly-ridden city made of salt slabs with camel skin roofs and entirely bereft of any trees. All food had to be brought in from outside, dates from the north and millet from the south. People travelled from the south to collect salt; in the words of Ibn Battuta (1929: 318):

The negroes use salt as a medium of exchange, just as gold and silver is used (elsewhere); they cut it up into pieces and buy and sell with it. The business done at Taghází, for all its meanness, amounts to an enormous figure in terms of hundredweights of gold-dust.

Travelling along the trade route that transferred gold from West Africa, Ibn Battuta provided posterity with not only a detailed itinerary but also a detailed description of the manner in which trade was conducted between the Mediterranean and West Africa.

The Asante Kingdom

The historian Ivor Wilks has convincingly demonstrated that it were smiths and traders from the Sahel, the area of the Sudanese states, who first discovered, developed and maintained the goldfields deep in the forests of present-day Côte d'Ivoire and Ghana (Wilks 1993: 1-39).

In the fifteenth century reports of the fabulous wealth of the ruler of Mali were known in Europe. Even before the completion of the 'Reconquista' of the Iberian peninsula in 1492 European powers not only gained extensive insight into the Almoravid kingdoms they had destroyed in mainland Europe, but they also sought to gain direct access to the trade in gold from West Africa which had been used in part to fund the establishment of the Muslim province of Al-Andalus in the peninsula. To this end, beginning in the 1450s Portuguese caravels began progressing ever further down the West African coast. By the 1460s they had passed and named Sierra Leone ('Lion Mountains'), and by 1471 had established Elmina ('the mine') on the Gold Coast (the present-day republic of Ghana).

The Portuguese had been anxious to find the true source of the gold of West Africa, to this end they had rounded Sierra Leone and tacked up the coast to where Elmina came to be situated. When they first cast anchor off the coast of

Ghana their hopes and aspirations appeared to have come about for they discovered coastal people who were prepared to trade in Gold and who used Malinke honorific titles to distinguish themselves. That is they had found people who were aware of 'Mali', and more importantly they had found, what appeared to be, another route to the gold of Mali that effectively bypassed the Sahara (Wilks 1993: 5).

The Portuguese began to import slaves from the kingdom of Benin – in present-day Nigeria – and the Congo to exchange in Elmina for gold, and at the beginning of the sixteenth century 'a yearly tally from 24,000 to 30,000 ounces' was being taken from Elmina to the treasury in Lisbon (Wilks 1993: 5). None the less, the Portuguese were aware of the fact that they were unable to compete sufficiently with the trade for gold from the forests northwards to the Sahel. The bulk of the forest gold travelled North through to Djenne on the Niger river, from where it was transported to Timbuktu and onwards across the Sahara.

In the mid-sixteenth century, Mande horsemen founded the kingdom of Gonja centred on Bighu between the Black and the White Volta, pushing the Mossi kingdom of Dagomba eastwards to modern Yendi (Isichei 1997: 230). According to Arab records the ruler of Mali had dispatched an expedition to Bighu to complain that tribute in gold was not reaching him. Instead of returning the soldiers established a new state, married into the local community and adopted the language of the people, whilst remaining the ruling caste.

Asante – golden stool

The newly established Gonja state appears to have relied on raiding for slaves, which it then exchanged with Akan polities in the forest region in exchange for Gold. Of these forest polities, the kingdom of Asante would rise to ascendancy at the end of the seventeenth century. Asante, imported slaves to dig for gold, raided slaves from the north and later came to export both. In the mid eighteenth century Bighu, which had once been subject to Mali, became a tributary state to Asante (Wilks 1993: 1-39).

Conclusion

For more than 1,500 years gold has determined the political economy of West Africa and determined its relations with the outside world. The horrors of the trans-Atlantic slave trade and the plantations of the New World are not to be ignored. Yet it must not be forgotten that the trans-Atlantic slave trade lasted for a comparatively short period of time, approximately three hundred years. Furthermore, the bulk of literature dealing with the Slave Trade concentrates on what occurred outside of Africa, and when it does deal with Africa and its peoples, they are presented as victims duped and subjected to the will of calculating foreigners. Indeed, this sad nihilistic history obscures more than that it illuminates, Africans are presented as victims robbed of agency. It is a history that hides the far longer and richer history of West African gold, the bulk of which, prior to the introduction of industrial technology in the early 1900s, was dug and mined by agriculturalists in those seasons of the year in which no work was needed on their fields. This West African gold powered the global economy centred on Europe and the Indian Ocean prior to the discovery of gold in the Americas. West African gold, dug by agriculturalists, underwrote the caliphates of North Africa, Arabia, Asia and Southern Europe following the Islamic conquest. The lure of West African gold powered the voyages of exploration emanating from the Iberian peninsula. From 1500 onwards West African gold would power the world system that came to be established and which would come to encompass the whole world. Underlying all of these momentous events were millions of agriculturalists who searched for gold when the agricultural cycle provided them with the time and the space to do so. Social forms and structures associated with the Mande speaking peoples of West Africa provided a template within which gold could be dealt with. A template that remained in existence and only came to be transgressed in the twentieth century with the introduction of highly financed industrial mining enterprises. For at least 1,500 years gold dug by West African agriculturalists has shaped global history, it is a history that outshines the dark nihilism of Africa's victimhood.

The Indian gold

MINING OF GOLD

Mining of gold is perhaps as old as the human civilization in India. It is reasonable
to believe that the small-scale mining or working of alluvial placer gold deposits
preceded vein gold mining in ancient India. This hypothesis gets credence in
view of the fact that the Vedic civilization was river based, and the people must
have noticed the shining nuggets and particles of gold in the sand and' gravels
of rivers. However, the concurrent working of these two types of deposits must
also have continued throughout the ages.

Unfortunately, the literary evidences of the ancient alluvial placer gold mining are
very few, and that too are not "direct" ones. As stated earlier, many rivers of India
in ancient times have been stated to have gold, indirectly referring to the
availability of alluvial placer gold from these rivers. It has also been stated earlier
that the names of many rivers in ancient India started with the word meaning
gold. This is another indirect evidence of the availability of alluvial placer gold in
these rivers.

DEPOSITS OF GOLD IN ANCIENT INDIA

In the Atharvaveda, the earth has been referred to `hiranyavaksa', i.e., the one
containing gold in her chest -

/ •

visvambhara vasudhani pratistha hiroyavaksa jagato nivesanr I

vagvanararb bibhrati bhamiragnimindrarishbha dravine no dadhatull

(Atharvaveda, 12.1.6)

The above hymn implies that the earth has mines of gold. The word thumi' in the above hymn does not denote merely the surface of the plain land, but it also includes banks and beds of rivers, hills_ of mountains, together with the interior of the earth.

In ancient India, the following types of gold deposits were known-:..

1. Alluvial Placer Deposit

2. Vein Deposit, and

3. "Liquid" Ore

India's Contribution to the Mining, Extraction and Refining of Gold...

Alluvial' Placer Deposit

There is a considerable amount of reference to the alluvial placer deposit of gold and the recovery of gold from such deposits. The Rgveda (10.75.8) mentions that the river Sindhu (Indus) contains gold —

"This is the river Sindhu which is full of horses, chariots, cotton, gold, grains, and wool these materials are either produced or found on the banks or the nearby area of the river Sindhu).

Its banks contain ropelike plants which are used to tie down ploughs. It bestows fortune on people, and such plants are grown on its banks that help in producing greater amount of honey".

Vein Deposit

Vein deposits are the important deposits of gold. The rocks of mountains are the important source of vein deposits of. gold.

The Ramayana mentions various mountains, which contained gold. These were: Udai and Saumanasa mountains in the eastern, Soma, Pariyatra and Varaha mountains in the western, and Kala mountain in the northern direction of India.

In the Mahabharata (Vana, -104.2), it has been stated that the Meru or Sumeru mountain contained gold.

The Liquid Ore of Gold

However, it is possible to visualize the chemical processes which must have been responsible for the

dissolution of gold in nature into the liquids available in its surroundings under

specific conditions. Some of these are discussed below.

Gold may be complexed and rendered soluble by the products of certain organic

compounds, e.g., I-12S produced by bacteria that gives rise to [AuS][131. The

oxidation of sulphides and sulphosalts may produce a variety of species such as

fthiosulphate, sulphite, polythionate and sulphate depending upon the Eh and

pH[13]. A number of other complexes may also be formed, e.g., HS-, HS03, HS-0 species, etc.[13]. .Gold may dissolve in many of these species forming

complexes such as [AuS]-, [Au(HS)2r, [Au(S203)2]3-, [Au(S03)23--, [Au(SO4)2]-, etc.

Gold may also dissolve as chloro complexes, as per the following reactiont131.

$2Au° + 2H+ + 4Cl--\longrightarrow 2[AuCl2J- + H2$

Ferric salts such as sulphates dissolve gold in the presence of dissolved chlorides

under the acidic conditiont131. The ferric ion renders the gold in an oxidized state,

which then combines with the chloride to form soluble complexes —

$Fe3++Au° Fe2+ + Au+$

$Au+ + 201--\longrightarrow [AuC12]-$

used in ancient times.

Several old old workings have' been reported in the Dharwar area of South India. Important old gold workings have been found between the town of Gadag and the river Tungabhadra by several workers. Maclaren[16]has mentioned two dozen pits of 18-25 ft in depth on the top of Jalgaragudd Hill (Goldwasher's Hill). He has described the old workings as often characterized by no more than shallow depressions where the grass was greener; all that remained of a pit of 80-100 ft in vertical depth. The upper part of the old workings had been packed with large rocks and debris after the work was complete.

Evidence of ancient mining

Timber, semi-charred timber, ashes and iron gouges have been found in many of these old gold workings. Timbering was used in supporting the galleries, and length of babul (Acacia arabica) were found. Some of the babul lengths had the irregular marks of adze cutting, while some had been rounded off at the ends to fit into uprights. The availability of timber, semi charred timber and ashes in old workings point towards the fact that rock faces were fire set, which were subsequently quenched with water. This enabled the rocks to fracture which subsequently fell into pieces. Alternatively, the fracturing of rocks makes easy breaking of hard rocks from the main body. At depth of hundreds of feet in some old workings, the deposit of as much as 10 ft of broken water pots at the bottom of old workings has been reported. This indicates that here the miners came across a spring, and further mining was abandoned in the shaft.

Munn (1997) has observed that the upper parts of the old workings had been carefully hand-packed with large rocks and debris after any section was completed. Munn suggests that this was done with a view to prevent the surface water to flow into the mine, and perhaps also to prevent the collapse of the excavation. He is also of the view that the ancient miners were doing it to conceal the mines from the observation of invaders in time of war.

In 1955 AD C14 analysis of two specimens of timber found at a depth of about 250 feet- in the old workings at Oakleys, shaft of Hutti mine were carried out in

New Zealand.

The results were as -follows:

Sample No. 1 — 1890 + 70 years

BP and Sample No. 2 — 1810 + 70 years BC

All the dates of other objects, such as small pots of coarse pink-red earth ware, cylindrical grinding stone of pink sand stone, small stone discs of green chlorite schist, etc., found from the old workings and preserved at Hutti, which is in the range of 1st century BC to the 3rd century AD. This date is consistent with the dating suggested by the C14 analysis. The above archaeological evidences from the Hutti field suggest that the gold mines were being worked at depths of 250 feet during the 1st century of the Christian era.

Based on the above description of old gold workings, one may reconstruct the method employed in the mines of Hutti in ancient times, which may be considered as a representation of the method used in other areas also. The various steps used in deep mining were as follows. The first step consisted of going down the dip of the reef with a small shaft or series of shafts. The ore was extracted laterally from the shaft resulting in a flat back open overhand Stope.

Excavation was achieved by means of fire setting. Auriferous rock was removed and hauled to the surface in bags or baskets by ropes and windlasses for the recovery of gold.

This is supported by the appearance of smooth sides of the rock face in the shafts caused due to prolonged rubbing with ropes, as observed in old workings.

Timbers were used for supporting the galleries. The water from spring foundation greater depth of mines was hauled to the surface by means of water pots.

Neolithic period.

He has-stated that the first discovery of gold bearing reefs was during the Neolithic period, which in the Deccan is now established at between the end of the 3rd millennium BC and the first half of the 1st millennium BC.

The mining work in this period would have mainly on the surface, i.e., open cast mining and alluvial placer gold mining. The tools available were too limited for any deep mining: stone picks are found in local Neolithic assemblages. However, due to availability of gold people started settling near the gold fields. On the

basis of archaeological findings, small scale and local extraction of gold was taking place in the Neolithic period in the Wandalli and Hutti zones. The next stage must have been marked with the arrival of tools

made of carburized steel, which must have increased the scale of operation.

EXTRACTION OF GOLD

The recovery of gold from the alluvial placer, this process consisted of agitating the auriferous sand along with water in a pan. The lighter sand particles were drained out along with water, leaving behind heavier gold particles and some residual sand. This rougher concentrate was further panned several times resulting into gold dust having very little sand or other impurities. The persons engaged in gold washing were called "pansudhavaka", and were different from goldsmith.

The basic process for the recovery of gold from alluvial placer deposit, popularly known as gold washing, has not changed since the antiquity, although some details must have been changing with time and place of operation.

Gold washing process may be summarized as follows.

Early recovery methods for gold from alluvial placer deposit were based upon the use of dish shaped pans made of wood or iron, and the technique was known as panning. The techniques differ according to custom and pan design.

Most pans have one common characteristic — a large internal surface area and shallow depth. Basically, however, all methods relied upon a thorough puddling 'of the alluvial placer deposit mass by hand and agitation, using an oscillatory motion. As a result, the heavier gold particles settled preferentially. A swirling motion of the pan under water continuously washed the top layer of light particles away until only a small amount remains. This rougher concentrate is a mixture of gold particles and lighter sand or mineral particles. Rougher concentrates from various runs were collected and further panned to a product in which the percentage of gold was high. Repeated panning resulted into gold dust having very little sand or other impurities. However, the success of the process greatly depended upon the skill of the washer. Alternatively, the gold and sand mixture were subjected to amalgamation, wherein gold combined with mercury, which was separated from the sand. The amalgam was heated in a suitable container to evaporate mercury, leaving behind gold.

If the alluvial placer deposit contained very coarse size gravels and pebbles, then the deposit was put over a sieve, made of bamboo or similar material, laid over a trough. Water was poured upon the heap of deposit, and the deposit was stirred until all the sand was carried through the sieve into the trough. The remaining coarse particles lying on the sieve were rejected. The sand collected in the trough was panned for gold, as described earlier.

The run-of-mine gold ores obtained either from the open cast mining or deep mining was crushed in the batteries of crushers on the ground level. Several explorers have noticed the evidence of such crushers near many old gold workings.

Understanding the gold standard

"[W]e don't have the gold standard. It's not because we don't know about the gold standard, it's because we do." Allan H. Meltzer

The gold standard is a monetary system where a country's currency or paper money has a value directly linked to gold. With the gold standard, countries agreed to convert paper money into a fixed amount of gold. A country that uses the gold standard sets a fixed price for gold and buys and sells gold at that price. That fixed price is used to determine the value of the currency. For example, if the U.S. sets the price of gold at $500 an ounce, the value of the dollar would be 1/500th of an ounce of gold.

The gold standard is not currently used by any government. Britain stopped using the gold standard in 1931 and the U.S. followed suit in 1933 and abandoned the remnants of the system in 1971. The gold standard was completely replaced by fiat money, a term to describe currency that is used because of a government's order, or fiat, that the currency must be accepted as a means of payment. In the U.S., for instance, the dollar is fiat money, and for Nigeria, it is the naira.

The appeal of a gold standard is that it arrests control of the issuance of money out of the hands of imperfect human beings. With the physical quantity of gold acting as a limit to that issuance, a society can follow a simple rule to avoid the evils of inflation. The goal of monetary policy is not just to prevent inflation, but also deflation, and to help promote a stable monetary environment in which full employment can be achieved. A brief history of the U.S. gold standard is enough to show that when such a simple rule is adopted, inflation can be avoided, but strict adherence to that rule can create economic instability, if not political unrest.

Origin

The gold specie standard arose from the widespread acceptance of gold as currency.[5] Various commodities have been used as money; typically, the one that loses the least value over time becomes the accepted form. Chemically, gold is of all major metals the one most resistant to corrosion.[citation needed]

The use of gold as money began thousands of years ago in Asia Minor.

During the early and high Middle Ages, the Byzantine gold solidus, commonly known as the bezant, was used widely throughout Europe and the Mediterranean. However, as the Byzantine Empire's economic influence declined, so too did the use of the bezant. In its place, European territories chose silver as their currency over gold, leading to the development of silver standards.

Silver pennies based on the Roman denarius became the staple coin of Mercia in Great Britain around the time of King Offa, circa 757–796 CE.[9] Similar coins, including Italian denari, French deniers, and Spanish dineros, circulated in Europe. Spanish explorers discovered silver deposits in Mexico in 1522 and at Potosí in Bolivia in 1545.[10] International trade came to depend on coins such as the Spanish dollar, the Maria Theresa thaler, and, later, the United States trade dollar.

In modern times, the British West Indies was one of the first regions to adopt a gold specie standard. Following Queen Anne's proclamation of 1704, the British West Indies gold standard was a de facto gold standard based on the Spanish gold doubloon. In 1717, Sir Isaac Newton, the master of the Royal Mint, established a new mint ratio between silver and gold that had the effect of driving silver out of circulation and putting Britain on a gold standard.[11][self-published source]

A formal gold specie standard was first established in 1821, when Britain adopted it following the introduction of the gold sovereign by the new Royal Mint at Tower Hill in 1816. The United Province of Canada in 1854, Newfoundland in 1865, and the United States and Germany (de jure) in 1873 adopted gold. The United States used the eagle as its unit, Germany introduced the new gold mark, while Canada adopted a dual system based on both the American gold eagle and the British gold sovereign.[12]

Australia and New Zealand adopted the British gold standard, as did the British West Indies, while Newfoundland was the only British Empire territory to introduce its own gold coin.[13] Royal Mint branches were established in Sydney, Melbourne, and Perth for the purpose of minting gold sovereigns from Australia's rich gold deposits.

The gold specie standard came to an end in the United Kingdom and the rest of the British Empire with the outbreak of World War I.[14]

Silver

From 1750 to 1870, wars within Europe as well as an ongoing trade deficit with China (which sold to Europe but had little use for European goods) drained silver from the economies of Western Europe and the United States. Coins were struck in smaller and smaller numbers, and there was a proliferation of bank and stock notes used as money.

United Kingdom

In the 1790s, the United Kingdom suffered a silver shortage. It ceased to mint larger silver coins and instead issued "token" silver coins and overstruck foreign coins. With the end of the Napoleonic Wars, the Bank of England began the massive recoinage programme that created standard gold sovereigns, circulating crowns, half-crowns and eventually copper farthings in 1821. The recoinage of silver after a long drought produced a burst of coins. The United Kingdom struck nearly 40 million shillings between 1816 and 1820, 17 million half crowns and 1.3 million silver crowns.

The 1819 Act for the Resumption of Cash Payments set 1823 as the date for resumption of convertibility, which was reached by 1821. Throughout the 1820s, small notes were issued by regional banks. This was restricted in 1826, while the Bank of England was allowed to set up regional branches. In 1833 however, Bank of England notes were made legal tender and redemption by other banks was discouraged. In 1844, the Bank Charter Act established that Bank of England notes were fully backed by gold and they became the legal standard. According to the strict interpretation of the gold standard, this 1844 act marked the establishment of a full gold standard for British money.

United States

In the 1780s, Thomas Jefferson, Robert Morris and Alexander Hamilton recommended to Congress the value of a decimal system. This system would also apply to monies in the United States. The question was what type of standard: gold, silver or both.[15] The United States adopted a silver standard based on the Spanish milled dollar in 1785.

International

From 1860 to 1871 various attempts to resurrect bi-metallic standards were made, including one based on the gold and silver franc; however, with the rapid influx of silver from new deposits, the expectation of scarce silver ended.

The interaction between central banking and currency basis formed the primary source of monetary instability during this period. The combination of a restricted supply of notes, a government monopoly on note issuance and indirectly, a central bank and a single unit of value produced economic stability. Deviation from these conditions produced monetary crises.

Devalued notes or leaving silver as a store of value caused economic problems. Governments, demanding specie as payment, could drain the money out of the economy. Economic development expanded need for credit. The need for a solid basis in monetary affairs produced a rapid acceptance of the gold standard in the period that followed.

Japan

Following Germany's decision after the 1870–1871 Franco-Prussian War to extract reparations to facilitate a move to the gold standard, Japan gained the needed reserves after the Sino-Japanese War of 1894–1895. For Japan, moving to gold was considered vital for gaining access to Western capital markets.[16]

Bimetallic standard

US: Pre-Civil War

In 1792, Congress passed the Mint and Coinage Act. It authorized the federal government's use of the Bank of the United States to hold its reserves, as well as establish a fixed ratio of gold to the U.S. dollar. Gold and silver coins were legal tender, as was the Spanish real. In 1792 the market price of gold was about 15 times that of silver.[15] Silver coins left circulation, exported to pay for the debts taken on to finance the American Revolutionary War. In 1806 President Jefferson suspended the minting of silver coins. This resulted in a derivative silver standard, since the Bank of the United States was not required to fully back its currency with reserves. This began a long series of attempts by the United States to create a bi-metallic standard.

The intention was to use gold for large denominations, and silver for smaller denominations. A problem with bimetallic standards was that the metals' absolute and relative market prices changed. The mint ratio (the rate at which the mint was obligated to pay/receive for gold relative to silver) remained fixed at 15 ounces of silver to 1 ounce of gold, whereas the market rate fluctuated from 15.5 to 1 to 16 to 1. With the Coinage Act of 1834, Congress passed an act that changed the mint ratio to approximately 16 to 1. Gold discoveries in California in 1848 and later in Australia lowered the gold price relative to silver; this drove silver money from circulation because it was worth more in the market than as money.[17] Passage of the Independent Treasury Act of 1848 placed the U.S. on a strict hard-money standard. Doing business with the American government required gold or silver coins.

Government accounts were legally separated from the banking system. However, the mint ratio (the fixed exchange rate between gold and silver at the mint) continued to overvalue gold. In 1853, the US reduced the silver weight of coins to keep them in circulation and in 1857 removed legal tender status from foreign coinage. In 1857 the final crisis of the free banking era began as American banks suspended payment in silver, with ripples through the developing international financial system. Due to the inflationary finance measures undertaken to help pay for the US Civil War, the government found it difficult to pay its obligations in gold or silver and suspended payments of obligations not legally specified in specie (gold bonds); this led banks to suspend the conversion of bank liabilities (bank notes and deposits) into specie. In 1862 paper money was made legal tender. It was a fiat money (not convertible on demand at a fixed rate into specie). These notes came to be called "greenbacks".[17]

US: Post-Civil War

After the Civil War, Congress wanted to reestablish the metallic standard at pre-war rates. The market price of gold in greenbacks was above the pre-War fixed price ($20.67 per ounce of gold) requiring deflation to achieve the pre-War price. This was accomplished by growing the stock of money less rapidly than real output. By 1879 the market price matched the mint price of gold. The coinage act of 1873 (also known as the Crime of '73) demonetized silver. This act removed the 412.5 grain silver dollar from circulation. Subsequently silver was only used in coins worth less than $1 (fractional currency). With the resumption of convertibility on June 30, 1879 the government again paid its debts in gold, accepted greenbacks for customs and redeemed greenbacks on demand in gold. Greenbacks were therefore perfect substitutes for gold coins. During the latter part of the nineteenth century the use of silver and a return to the bimetallic standard were recurrent political issues, raised especially by William Jennings Bryan, the People's Party and the Free Silver movement. In 1900 the gold dollar was declared the standard unit of account and a gold reserve for government issued paper notes was established. Greenbacks, silver certificates, and silver dollars continued to be legal tender, all redeemable in gold.[17]

Fluctuations in the US gold stock, 1862–1877

US gold stock

1862 59 tons

1866 81 tons

1875 50 tons

1878 78 tons

The US had a gold stock of 1.9 million ounces (59 t) in 1862. Stocks rose to 2.6 million ounces (81 t) in 1866, declined in 1875 to 1.6 million ounces (50 t) and rose to 2.5 million ounces (78 t) in 1878. Net exports did not mirror that pattern. In the decade before the Civil War net exports were roughly constant; postwar they varied erratically around pre-war levels, but fell significantly in 1877 and became negative in 1878 and 1879. The net import of gold meant that the foreign demand for American currency to purchase goods, services, and investments exceeded the corresponding American demands for foreign currencies. In the final years of the greenback period (1862–1879), gold production increased while gold exports decreased. The decrease in gold exports was considered by some to be a result of changing monetary conditions. The demands for gold during this period were as a speculative vehicle, and for its primary use in the foreign exchange markets financing international trade. The major effect of the increase in gold demand by the public and Treasury was to reduce exports of gold and increase the Greenback price of gold relative to purchasing power.[18]

Towards the end of the 19th century, some silver standard countries began to peg their silver coin units to the gold standards of the United Kingdom or the United States. In 1898, British India pegged the silver rupee to the pound sterling at a fixed rate of 1s 4d, while in 1906, the Straits Settlements adopted a gold exchange standard against sterling, fixing the silver Straits dollar at 2s 4d.

Around the start of the 20th century, the Philippines pegged the silver peso/dollar to the U.S. dollar at 50 cents. This move was assisted by the passage of the Philippines Coinage Act by the United States Congress on March 3, 1903.[19] Around the same time Mexico and Japan pegged their currencies to the dollar. When Siam adopted a gold exchange standard in 1908, only China and Hong Kong remained on the silver standard.

When adopting the gold standard, many European nations changed the name of their currency, for instance from Daler (Sweden and Denmark) or Gulden (Austria-Hungary) to Crown, since the former names were traditionally associated with silver coins and the latter with gold coins.

Impact of World War I

Governments with insufficient tax revenue suspended convertibility repeatedly in the 19th century. The real test, however, came in the form of World War I, a test which "it failed utterly" according to economist Richard Lipsey.[5]

By the end of 1913, the classical gold standard was at its peak but World War I caused many countries to suspend or abandon it.[20] According to Lawrence Officer the main cause of the gold standard's failure to resume its previous position after World War I was "the Bank of England's precarious liquidity position and the gold-exchange standard." A run on sterling caused Britain to impose exchange controls that fatally weakened the standard; convertibility was not legally suspended, but gold prices no longer played the role that they did before.[21] In financing the war and abandoning gold, many of the belligerents suffered drastic inflations. Price levels doubled in the US and Britain, tripled in France and quadrupled in Italy. Exchange rates changed less, even though European inflations were more severe than America's. This meant that the costs of American goods decreased relative to those in Europe. Between August 1914 and spring of 1915, the dollar value of US exports tripled and its trade surplus exceeded $1 billion for the first time.[22]

Ultimately, the system could not deal quickly enough with the large balance of payments deficits and surpluses; this was previously attributed to downward wage rigidity brought about by the advent of unionized labor, but is now considered as an inherent fault of the system that arose under the pressures of war and rapid technological change. In any case, prices had not reached equilibrium by the time of the Great Depression, which served to kill off the system completely.[5]

For example, Germany had gone off the gold standard in 1914, and could not effectively return to it because War reparations had cost it much of its gold reserves. During the Occupation of the Ruhr the German central bank (Reichsbank) issued enormous sums of non-convertible marks to support workers who were on strike against the French occupation and to buy foreign currency for reparations; this led to the German hyperinflation of the early 1920s and the decimation of the German middle class.

The US did not suspend the gold standard during the war. The newly created Federal Reserve intervened in currency markets and sold bonds to "sterilize" some of the gold imports that would have otherwise increased the stock of money.[citation needed] By 1927 many countries had returned to the gold standard.[17] As a result of World War I the United States, which had been a net debtor country, had become a net creditor by 1919.[23]

Abandonment of the gold standard

William McKinley ran for president on the basis of the gold standard.

The gold specie standard ended in the United Kingdom and the rest of the British Empire at the outbreak of World War I, when Treasury notes replaced the circulation of gold sovereigns and gold half sovereigns. Legally, the gold specie standard was not repealed. The end of the gold standard was successfully effected by the Bank of England through appeals to patriotism urging citizens not to redeem paper money for gold specie. It was only in 1925, when Britain returned to the gold standard in conjunction with Australia and South Africa, that the gold specie standard was officially ended.

The British Gold Standard Act 1925 both introduced the gold bullion standard and simultaneously repealed the gold specie standard. The new standard ended the circulation of gold specie coins. Instead, the law compelled the authorities to sell gold bullion on demand at a fixed price, but "only in the form of bars containing approximately four hundred ounces troy [12 kg] of fine gold".[24][25] John Maynard Keynes, citing deflationary dangers, argued against resumption of the gold standard.[26] By fixing the price at the pre-war rate of $4.86,[clarification needed] Churchill is argued to have made an error that led to depression, unemployment and the 1926 general strike. The decision was described by Andrew Turnbull as a "historic mistake".[27]

Many other countries followed Britain in returning to the gold standard, this was followed by a period of relative stability but also deflation.[28] This state of affairs lasted until the Great Depression (1929–1939) forced countries off the gold standard. In September 19, 1931, speculative attacks on the pound forced Britain to abandon the gold standard. Loans from American and French Central Banks of £50,000,000 were insufficient and exhausted in a matter of weeks, due to large gold outflows across the Atlantic.[29][30][31] The British benefited from this departure. They could now use monetary policy to stimulate the economy. Australia and New Zealand had already left the standard and Canada quickly followed suit.

The interwar partially backed gold standard was inherently unstable, because of the conflict between the expansion of liabilities to foreign central banks and the resulting deterioration in the Bank of England's reserve ratio. France was then attempting to make Paris a world class financial center, and it received large gold flows as well.[32]

In May 1931 a run on Austria's largest commercial bank caused it to fail. The run spread to Germany, where the central bank also collapsed. International financial assistance was too late and in July 1931 Germany adopted exchange controls, followed by Austria in October. The Austrian and German experiences, as well as British budgetary and political difficulties, were among the factors that destroyed confidence in sterling, which occurred in mid-July 1931. Runs ensued and the Bank of England lost much of its reserves.

Depression and World War II

Ending the gold standard and economic recovery during the Great Depression.[33]

Great Depression

Some economic historians, such as Barry Eichengreen, blame the gold standard of the 1920s for prolonging the economic depression which started in 1929 and lasted for about a decade.[34] In the United States, adherence to the gold standard prevented the Federal Reserve from expanding the money supply to stimulate the economy, fund insolvent banks and fund government deficits that could "prime the pump" for an expansion. Once off the gold standard, it became free to engage in such money creation. The gold standard limited the flexibility of the central banks' monetary policy by limiting their ability to expand the money supply. In the US, the central bank was required by the Federal Reserve Act (1913) to have gold backing 40% of its demand notes.[35] Others including former Federal Reserve Chairman Ben Bernanke and Nobel Prize-winner Milton Friedman place the blame for the severity and length of the Great Depression at the feet of the Federal Reserve, mostly due to the deliberate tightening of monetary policy even after the end of the gold standard.[36] They blamed the US major economic contraction in 1937 on tightening of monetary policy resulting in higher cost of capital, weaker securities markets, reduced net government contribution to income, the undistributed profits tax and higher labor costs.[37] The money supply peaked in March 1937, with a trough in May 1938.[38]

Higher interest rates intensified the deflationary pressure on the dollar and reduced investment in U.S. banks. Commercial banks converted Federal Reserve Notes to gold in 1931, reducing its gold reserves and forcing a corresponding reduction in the amount of currency in circulation. This speculative attack created a panic in the U.S. banking system. Fearing imminent devaluation many depositors withdrew funds from U.S. banks.[39] As bank runs grew, a reverse multiplier effect caused a contraction in the money supply.[40] Additionally the New York Fed had loaned over $150 million in gold (over 240 tons) to European Central Banks. This transfer contracted the US money supply. The foreign loans became questionable once Britain, Germany, Austria and other European countries went off the gold standard in 1931 and weakened confidence in the dollar.[41]

The forced contraction of the money supply resulted in deflation. Even as nominal interest rates dropped, deflation-adjusted real interest rates remained high, rewarding those who held onto money instead of spending it, further slowing the economy.[42] Recovery in the United States was slower than in Britain, in part due to Congressional reluctance to abandon the gold standard and float the U.S. currency as Britain had done.[43]

In the early 1930s, the Federal Reserve defended the dollar by raising interest rates, trying to increase the demand for dollars. This helped attract international investors who bought foreign assets with gold.[39]

Congress passed the Gold Reserve Act on 30 January 1934; the measure nationalized all gold by ordering Federal Reserve banks to turn over their supply to the U.S. Treasury. In return the banks received gold certificates to be used as reserves against deposits and Federal Reserve notes. The act also authorized the president to devalue the gold dollar. Under this authority the president, on 31 January 1934, changed the value of the dollar from $20.67 to the troy ounce to $35 to the troy ounce, a devaluation of over 40%.

Other factors in the prolongation of the Great Depression include trade wars and the reduction in international trade caused by barriers such as Smoot–Hawley Tariff in the US and the Imperial Preference policies of Great Britain,[44] the failure of central banks to act responsibly,[45] government policies designed to prevent wages from falling, such as the Davis–Bacon Act of 1931, during the deflationary period resulting in production costs dropping slower than sales prices, thereby injuring business profits[46] and increases in taxes to reduce budget deficits and to support new programs such as Social Security. The US top marginal income tax rate went from 25% to 63% in 1932 and to 79% in 1936,[47] while the bottom rate increased over tenfold, from .375% in 1929 to 4% in 1932.[48] The concurrent massive drought resulted in the US Dust Bowl.

The Austrian School asserted that the Great Depression was the result of a credit bust.[49] Alan Greenspan wrote that the bank failures of the 1930s were sparked by Great Britain dropping the gold standard in 1931. This act "tore asunder" any remaining confidence in the banking system.[50] Financial historian Niall Ferguson wrote that what made the Great Depression truly 'great' was the European banking crisis of 1931.[51] According to Fed Chairman Marriner Eccles, the root cause was the concentration of wealth resulting in a stagnating or decreasing standard of living for the poor and middle class. These classes went into debt, producing the credit explosion of the 1920s. Eventually the debt load grew too heavy, resulting in the massive defaults and financial panics of the 1930s.[52]

World War II

Under the Bretton Woods international monetary agreement of 1944, the gold standard was kept without domestic convertibility. The role of gold was severely constrained, as other countries' currencies were fixed in terms of the dollar. Many countries kept reserves in gold and settled accounts in gold. Still they preferred to settle balances with other currencies, with the American dollar becoming the favorite. The International Monetary Fund was established to help with the exchange process and assist nations in maintaining fixed rates. Within Bretton Woods adjustment was cushioned through credits that helped countries avoid deflation. Under the old standard, a country with an overvalued currency would lose gold and experience deflation until the currency was again valued correctly. Most countries defined their currencies in terms of dollars, but some countries imposed trading restrictions to protect reserves and exchange rates. Therefore, most countries' currencies were still basically inconvertible. In the late 1950s, the exchange restrictions were dropped and gold became an important element in international financial settlements.[17]

Bretton Woods

After the Second World War, a system similar to a gold standard and sometimes described as a "gold exchange standard" was established by the Bretton Woods Agreements. Under this system, many countries fixed their exchange rates relative to the U.S. dollar and central banks could exchange dollar holdings into gold at the official exchange rate of $35 per ounce; this option was not available to firms or individuals. All currencies pegged to the dollar thereby had a fixed value in terms of gold.[5]

Starting in the 1959–1969 administration of President Charles de Gaulle and continuing until 1970, France reduced its dollar reserves, exchanging them for gold at the official exchange rate, reducing US economic influence. This, along with the fiscal strain of federal expenditures for the Vietnam War and persistent balance of payments deficits, led U.S. President Richard Nixon to end international convertibility of the U.S. dollar to gold on August 15, 1971 (the "Nixon Shock").

This was meant to be a temporary measure, with the gold price of the dollar and the official rate of exchanges remaining constant. Revaluing currencies was the main purpose of this plan. No official revaluation or redemption occurred. The dollar subsequently floated. In December 1971, the "Smithsonian Agreement" was reached. In this agreement, the dollar was devalued from $35 per troy ounce of gold to $38. Other countries' currencies appreciated. However, gold convertibility did not resume. In October 1973, the price was raised to $42.22. Once again, the devaluation was insufficient. Within two weeks of the second devaluation the dollar was left to float. The $42.22 par value was made official in September 1973, long after it had been abandoned in practice. In October 1976, the government officially changed the definition of the dollar; references to gold were removed from statutes. From this point, the international monetary system was made of pure fiat money.

Production of gold

An estimated total of 174,100 tonnes of gold have been mined in human history, according to GFMS as of 2012. This is roughly equivalent to 5.6 billion troy ounces or, in terms of volume, about 9,261 cubic metres (327,000 cu ft), or a cube 21 metres (69 ft) on a side. There are varying estimates of the total volume of gold mined. One reason for the variance is that gold has been mined for thousands of years. Another reason is that some nations are not particularly open about how much gold is being mined. In addition, it is difficult to account for the gold output in illegal mining activities.[53]

World production for 2011 was circa 2,700 tonnes. Since the 1950s, annual gold output growth has approximately kept pace with world population growth (i.e. a doubling in this period)[54] although it has lagged behind world economic growth (approximately 8-fold increase since the 1950s[55], and 4x since 1980[56]).

Theory

Commodity money is inconvenient to store and transport in large amounts. Furthermore, it does not allow a government to manipulate the flow of commerce with the same ease that a fiat currency does. As such, commodity money gave way to representative money and gold and other specie were retained as its backing.

Gold was a preferred form of money due to its rarity, durability, divisibility, fungibility and ease of identification,[57] often in conjunction with silver. Silver was typically the main circulating medium, with gold as the monetary reserve. Commodity money was anonymous, as identifying marks can be removed. Commodity money retains its value despite what may happen to the monetary authority. After the fall of South Vietnam, many refugees carried their wealth to the West in gold after the national currency became worthless.[citation needed]

Under commodity standards currency itself has no intrinsic value, but is accepted by traders because it can be redeemed any time for the equivalent specie. A US silver certificate, for example, could be redeemed for an actual piece of silver.

Representative money and the gold standard protect citizens from hyperinflation and other abuses of monetary policy, as were seen in some countries during the Great Depression. Commodity money conversely led to deflation and bank runs.

Countries that left the gold standard earlier than other countries recovered from the Great Depression sooner. For example, Great Britain and the Scandinavian countries, which left the gold standard in 1931, recovered much earlier than France and Belgium, which remained on gold much longer. Countries such as China, which had a silver standard, almost entirely avoided the depression (due to the fact it was then barely integrated into the global economy). The connection between leaving the gold standard and the severity and duration of the depression was consistent for dozens of countries, including developing countries. This may explain why the experience and length of the depression differed between national economies.[58]

Variations

A full or 100%-reserve gold standard exists when the monetary authority holds enough gold to convert all the circulating representative money into gold at the promised exchange rate. It is sometimes referred to as the gold specie standard to more easily distinguish it. Opponents of a full standard consider it difficult to implement, saying that the quantity of gold in the world is too small to sustain worldwide economic activity at or near current gold prices; implementation would entail a many-fold increase in the price of gold.[citation needed] Gold standard proponents have said, "Once a money is established, any stock of money becomes compatible with any amount of employment and real income."[59] While prices would necessarily adjust to the supply of gold, the process may involve considerable economic disruption, as was experienced during earlier attempts to maintain gold standards.[60]

In an international gold-standard system (which is necessarily based on an internal gold standard in the countries concerned),[61] gold or a currency that is convertible into gold at a fixed price is used to make international payments. Under such a system, when exchange rates rise above or fall below the fixed mint rate by more than the cost of shipping gold, inflows or outflows occur until rates return to the official level. International gold standards often limit which entities have the right to redeem currency for gold.

Advantages

Long-term price stability has been described as one of the virtues of the gold standard.[62] The gold standard makes it difficult for governments to inflate prices through expanding the money supply. Under the gold standard, significant inflation is rare, and hyperinflation is essentially impossible because the money supply can only grow at the rate that the gold supply increases. High inflation under a gold standard is seen only when warfare destroys a large part of an economy, reducing the production of goods, or when a major new gold source becomes available.[63] In the U.S., inflation occurred during the Civil War, which destroyed the economy of the South.[64] Inflation also followed the California Gold Rush that made large amounts of gold available for minting.[65] Historical data shows that the magnitude of short run swings in prices were far higher under the gold standard.[66][62]

The gold standard provides fixed international exchange rates between participating countries and thus reduces uncertainty in international trade. Historically, imbalances between price levels were offset by a balance-of-payment adjustment mechanism called the "price–specie flow mechanism".[63] Gold used to pay for imports reduces the money supply of importing nations, causing deflation, which makes them more competitive, while the importation of gold by net exporters serves to increase their money supply, causing inflation, making them less competitive.[67]

A gold standard does not allow some types of financial repression.[68] Financial repression acts as a mechanism to transfer wealth from creditors to debtors, particularly the governments that practice it. Financial repression is most successful in reducing debt when accompanied by inflation and can be considered a form of taxation.[69][70] In 1966 Alan Greenspan wrote "Deficit spending is simply a scheme for the confiscation of wealth. Gold stands in the way of this insidious process. It stands as a protector of property rights. If one grasps this, one has no difficulty in understanding the statists' antagonism toward the gold standard."[71]

Disadvantages

Gold prices (US$ per troy ounce) from 1914, in nominal US$ and inflation adjusted US$.

The unequal distribution of gold deposits makes the gold standard more advantageous for those countries that produce gold.[72] In 2010 the largest producers of gold, in order, were China, Australia, U.S., South Africa and Russia.[73] The country with the largest unmined gold deposits is Australia.[74]

Some economists believe that the gold standard acts as a limit on economic growth. "As an economy's productive capacity grows, then so should its money supply. Because a gold standard requires that money be backed in the metal, then the scarcity of the metal constrains the ability of the economy to produce more capital and grow."[75]

Mainstream economists believe that economic recessions can be largely mitigated by increasing the money supply during economic downturns.[76] A gold standard means that the money supply would be determined by the gold supply and hence monetary policy could no longer be used to stabilize the economy.[77] The gold standard is often blamed for prolonging the Great Depression, as under the gold standard, central banks could not expand credit at a fast enough rate to offset deflationary forces.[78]

Although the gold standard brings long-run price stability, it is historically associated with high short-run price volatility.[62][79] It has been argued by Schwartz, among others, that instability in short-term price levels can lead to financial instability as lenders and borrowers become uncertain about the value of debt.[79]

Deflation punishes debtors.[80][81] Real debt burdens therefore rise, causing borrowers to cut spending to service their debts or to default. Lenders become wealthier, but may choose to save some of the additional wealth, reducing GDP.[82]

The money supply would essentially be determined by the rate of gold production. When gold stocks increase more rapidly than the economy, there is inflation and the reverse is also true.[62][83] The consensus view is that the gold standard contributed to the severity and length of the Great Depression.[84][85]

Hamilton contended that the gold standard is susceptible to speculative attacks when a government's financial position appears weak. Conversely, this threat discourages governments from engaging in risky policy (see moral hazard). For example, the U.S. was forced to contract the money supply and raise interest rates in September 1931 to defend the dollar after speculators forced the UK off the gold standard.[85][86][87][88]

Devaluing a currency under a gold standard would generally produce sharper changes than the smooth declines seen in fiat currencies, depending on the method of devaluation.[89]

Most economists favor a low, positive rate of inflation of around 2%. This reflects fear of deflationary shocks and the belief that active monetary policy can dampen fluctuations in output and unemployment. Inflation gives them room to tighten policy without inducing deflation.[90]

A gold standard provides practical constraints against the measures that central banks might otherwise use to respond to economic crises.[91] Creation of new money reduces interest rates and thereby increases demand for new lower cost debt, raising the demand for money.[92]

Advocates

A return to the gold standard was considered by the US Gold Commission back in 1982, but found only minority support.[93] In 2001 Malaysian Prime Minister Mahathir bin Mohamad proposed a new currency that would be used initially for international trade among Muslim nations, using a Modern Islamic gold dinar, defined as 4.25 grams of pure (24-carat) gold. Mahathir claimed it would be a stable unit of account and a political symbol of unity between Islamic nations. This would purportedly reduce dependence on the US dollar and establish a non-debt-backed currency in accord with Sharia law that prohibited the charging of interest.[94] As of 2013 the global monetary system continued to rely on the US dollar as the main reserve currency.[95]

Former U.S. Federal Reserve Chairman, Alan Greenspan acknowledged he was one of "a small minority" within the central bank that had some positive view on the gold standard.[96] In a 1966 essay he contributed to a book by Ayn Rand, titled "Gold and Economic Freedom", Greenspan argued the case for returning to a 'pure' gold standard; in that essay he described supporters of fiat currencies as "welfare statists" intending to use monetary policy to finance deficit spending.[97] More recently he claimed that by focusing on targeting inflation "central bankers have behaved as though we were on the gold standard", rendering a return to the standard unnecessary.[98]

Similarly, economists like Robert Barro argued that whilst some form of "monetary constitution" is essential for stable, depoliticized monetary policy, the form this constitution takes—for example, a gold standard, some other commodity-based standard, or a fiat currency with fixed rules for determining the quantity of money—is considerably less important.[99]

The gold standard is supported by many followers of the Austrian School of Economics, free-market libertarians and some supply-siders.[100]

US politics

In the United States, strict constitutionalists object to the government issuing fiat currency through central banks. Some gold-standard advocates also call for a mandated end to fractional-reserve banking. Many similar alternatives have been suggested, including energy-based currencies, collections of currencies or commodities, with gold as one component.

Former congressman Ron Paul is a long-term, high-profile advocate of a gold standard, but has also expressed support for using a standard based on a basket of commodities that better reflects the state of the economy.[101]

In 2011 the Utah legislature passed a bill to accept federally issued gold and silver coins as legal tender to pay taxes.[102] As federally issued currency, the coins were already legal tender for taxes, although the market price of their metal content currently exceeds their monetary value. Similar legislation is under consideration in other US states.[103] The bill was initiated by newly elected Republican Party legislators associated with the Tea Party movement and was driven by anxiety over the policies of President Barack Obama.[104]

In 2013, the Arizona Legislature passed SB 1439, which would have made gold and silver coin a legal tender in payment of debt, but the bill was vetoed by the Governor.[105]

In 2015, some candidates for the 2016 presidential election advocated for a gold standard, based on concern that the Federal Reserve's attempts to increase economic growth may create inflation. Economic historians did not agree with candidate's assertions that the gold standard would benefit the US economy.[106]

Critics

In 2012 a poll of 40 U.S. economists in the IGM Economic Experts Panel found that none of them believed returning to the gold standard would result in "price-stability and employment outcomes [that] would be better for the average American." The panel of polled economists included past Nobel Prize winners, former economic advisers to both Republican and Democratic presidents, and senior faculty from Harvard, Chicago, Stanford, MIT, and other well-known research universities. The specific statement with which the economists were asked to agree or disagree was as follows: "If the US replaced its discretionary monetary policy regime with a gold standard, defining a 'dollar' as a specific number of ounces of gold, the price-stability and employment outcomes would be better for the average American."[3]

How Global Trade Made Men Wealthy during the California Gold Rush

On May 12, 1848, a store owner named Sam Brannan held a "one-man parade" to announce the start of the San Francisco Gold Rush.

"Gold! Gold from the American River!" Brannan shouted up and down Market Street in San Francisco. He held his hat in one hand and waved a bottle of gold dust in the other. San Franciscans had received false news of gold before. But by all accounts, Brannan's performance sent residents running in search of riches.

Brannan had a good reason for spreading the news rather than panning for gold himself. The canny entrepreneur owned a general store that served the workers at Sutter's Mill, the site where gold was discovered. And in the week between learning about the discovery and yelling about it in San Francisco, he'd bought all the picks and shovels in the city.

Brannan's announcement helped spur a seminal event in California's history. As Brannan raked in money selling mining supplies, his actions also, years later, led to the coining of a famous maxim: During a gold rush, sell shovels.

It's true that most miners fared poorly during the Gold Rush. But the men and women who prospered the most tended to ignore gold in favor of another resource: the hundreds of thousands of new arrivals who transformed an isolated frontier into a prosperous and industrialized population center in less than a decade.

"California needed everything and had nothing," Edward D. Businessmen and women who grasped this profited enormously from trade and the flow of goods and people to the new promised land.

Rather than advising someone to sell shovels and pick axes during a gold rush, better advice from the San Francisco Gold Rush might be to import shovels from abroad. Or speculate in real estate. Or just work hard painting houses. Anything but mining for gold.

1848-1850: The Growth of the "Golden City"

The San Francisco Bay Area has been so thoroughly tamed by highways, cities, and sprawl that it's hard to appreciate how recently the area was wild frontier.

When traders visited the area in the 1830s, they published descriptions of California in newspapers to satisfy Americans' desire to learn about this far-off Eden. The Bay Area consisted mostly of ranches, missions, and the occasional fort; the dominant trade was of cow hides and animal fat in exchange for clothes, food, and household goods. Before the Gold Rush, the entire population of California was 14,000. San Francisco was a small settlement of some 500 people.

The Bay Area simply had not had the time or density to develop infrastructure. There were no bridges across rivers or roads between towns. "The only wagons," Dolnick writes in The Rush, "were carts with solid, wooden, Flintstone-style wheels a foot thick."

This meant that the Bay Area was as hard to reach as a far-off island. Letters from the president to his representative in California took six months to arrive by ship. In the 1840s, explorers were still searching out good overland routes across the Sierras to California, and sailing from the East Coast around the tip of South America to San Francisco or Monterey was a dangerous, months-long voyage.

In 1848, politicians and businessmen had no doubt that San Francisco had a grand future. America was in the grip of Manifest Destiny, going to war to wrest control of California and the Southwest from Mexico, and the natural port provided by the Bay made it a natural spot for development.

They just expected it to take time due to San Francisco's isolation and the scale of the unsettled West. When Mexico and Spain controlled the area, their governments had struggled to convince people to move to the Bay because better farmland was available closer to Mexico.

The Gold Rush, however, dramatically sped up this process.

Nearly 200,000 people arrived in California in 1849 and 1850. California entered the union (United States) and became the 31st state on September 1850. In a few short years, over 1% of America's population made the trek in search of fortune, quickly turning San Francisco into a massive construction site and a swashbuckling city where barbers looked for gold flakes in their patrons trimmed whiskers. Excluding world wars, it was the largest migration of American men in history.

And the people most involved in transporting these people and the goods they needed profited enormously.

A Monopoly on California

The American Transcontinental Railroad famous linked the Atlantic Ocean to the Pacific in 1869—well after the discovery of gold in California. But in 1855, a railway in Panama began running from sea to shining sea.

The railway was the creation of three American businessmen, one of whom already ran steam ships to and from Panamanian ports on the Atlantic and Pacific. In his mind, building a railroad would allow him to link New York and California— and control the crucial link between the oceans.

It was an alluring thought, and in the late 1840s, the men raised one million dollars (perhaps $30 million in today's dollars) to fund their idea. Although the Panama Canal would not be built until 1914, people already used Panama as a shortcut across the continent. Once the Gold Rush began, cutting through Panama became a common route from the East Coast to California.

It was a dangerous journey. The path across Panama, where the railroad would be built, was dense jungle. In good conditions, people headed to California could cross in a week by taking a dugout canoe—pushed along by nearly naked boatmen who shocked Americans' delicate sensibilities—followed by a 20 mile journey through the mountains on mules.

An easy crossing was merely uncomfortable. During bad crossings, the way became a "river of mud" and diseases like cholera killed dozens of people. Historian David McCullough writes that Ulysses S. Grant, who made the crossing in 1852 to take up a military post in California, "would talk more of the horrors he had seen in Panama than of any battles he had known."

The three men financing and constructing the Panama Railway knew very little about railroads, which is probably the only reason the railway was built. In the unfriendly Panamanian terrain, the men exhausted their capital in a year and laid only 7 miles of track. But the frenzied gold seekers saved the project.

The hundreds of thousands of people headed to California desired nothing more than speed. In 1851, a group of migrants asked to use the seven-mile track to speed their Panamanian crossing. The railroad owners realized they could profitably run trains on their unfinished railway, and the profits from the new passengers, along with new investment from Wall Street, paid for the $8 million construction project that still awes engineers to this day.

When the engineers hammered the last spike to finish the railway in 1855, the company had already been profitable for years. Soon it became the most highly valued company on the New York Stock Exchange. It took a small cut of the value of all cargo, and people returning from California took $500 million worth of gold on the railway in just 10 years.

When the railway opened, the office in Colon jokingly sent the head office in New York a rate card suggesting absurdly high prices. But as David McCullough writes in an authoritative profile, managers in New York took it seriously and charged passengers $300 (in today's dollars).

"The explanation was obvious enough, David McCullough . "The road had a total monopoly on the isthmian transit, and until the completion of the Union Pacific [Transcontinental Railroad] in 1869, it had no competition for the California traffic."

They essentially had a monopoly on the road to El Dorado for 14 years.

Winning the Gold Rush

Although America's "Wild West" period has been dramatized and romanticized, the insanity of the Gold Rush is no exaggeration. It really was bonkers.

Many accounts describe how seemingly everyone ran toward the gold fields with or without tools and food. And it was literally everyone. Businessmen wrote letters noting that the wealthy had to do their own cooking and cleaning because the help all left. San Francisco's port filled with ships whose crews abandoned them on reaching the city, so people just built wharfs that extended past them. One Census found that the Bay Area had 624 miners for every 1000 people.

Yet among these adventure stories of people crossing continents, winning and losing fortunes in the course of days, many of the Californians who emerged as its richest denizens, like Thomas Larkin and Faxon Dean Atherton, were conservative businessmen.

When Atherton heard about the discovery of gold in California, he reacted with skepticism and wrote that he hoped coal would be discovered. He was an American merchant in Chile who traded with California, and he did not move to California until 1860. (Although once he did, he moved to a town that ultimately took his name, Atherton, and thanks to the technology "gold rush" of the last 50 years, became one of the wealthiest areas in Silicon Valley.)

Atherton was friends and often business partners with Thomas Larkin, a businessman who had served as consul to Mexico before America assumed control of California. Larkin was an ambitious man, but he did not fall for gold fever even as his letters to D.C. helped spark the Gold Rush. He lamented that his workers left for the gold mines, and he wrote of the gold discovery, "The future consequence or prospect is not pleasant or moral."

But the Gold Rush made both of these humbugs rich. They made only modest investments in gold mining or selling mining equipment. Instead, as their biographers write, they recognized the business potential of serving tens of thousands of new settlers.

One of Larkin's first lucrative moves was financing voyages that brought clothes and food to San Francisco. Ship captains bought goods using tens of thousands of dollars on credit from Larkin in China, Mexico, and other Pacific ports, and Larkin also played middleman by buying entire ships' cargoes when they arrived in San Francisco. A number of his ventures doubled his investment in a few months.

Larkin and Atherton enjoyed a profitable friendship, so Atherton profited by using information from Larkin to arrange voyages from his perch in Chile to this new, lucrative market in San Francisco. By the time he moved to California in 1860, he, along with Larkin, had become some of the state's richest men from this trade.

"He had the dreamer's eye; the realist's wisdom," a biographer wrote of Atherton. "He was one of those unsung men of business who labored to build an economic foundation on which the settler, gold miner, rancher, and shopkeeper were dependent for goods and capital investment."

Even as men were digging up chunks of gold weighing as much as 195 pounds from California's riverbeds, Atherton and Larkin became two of the state's richest men by following a strategy "built on essential elements: foodstuffs, dependable commodities, and investment in land."

The Real Source of Wealth - People

In 1849, California did not have the population to qualify for statehood, and the mining towns springing up consisted of tents and wooden shacks that burned down every few months. A few years later, San Francisco had stately streets and a soaring population.

In the early, mining-centric economy, selling shovels was a good business. Sam Brannan, the man who held the "one-man parade" shouting "gold!", quickly made a killing selling picks and shovels and staking gold miners. Levi Strauss famously became rich by selling jeans, which appealed to miners because Strauss reinforced the pockets with rivets.

But the people who profited most from the Gold Rush didn't necessarily "sell shovels"—literally or metaphorically.

Although Brannan allegedly became California's first millionaire, the real secret to his wealth was moving up from selling shovels to speculating in real estate (he bought much of modern-day Sacramento when it was still a "muddy landing at a river junction") and banking (he lobbied furiously against a ban on commercial banking in California).

The California Gold Rush led to such rapid growth and such ubiquitous demand that a determined person could make good money doing just about anything— except mining gold. "Everyone must do something, it matters but very little what it is," one settler wrote. "If they stick to it, they are bound to make money."

While miners endured hardship for wages that were no better than those they'd earned at home—a condition they accepted for the chance of instant riches— 49ers who abandoned their golden dreams steadily accumulated modest riches painting houses, stitching clothes and baking pies. In today's money, a farmer selling onions made $160,000 in 1849; some deliverymen made six-figure salaries.

Areas from China to Hawaii to Mexico experienced inflation and shortages as merchants rushed goods to this massive, new Californian market. During the rush, settlers created entire industries from scratch—in ironworks, lumber, and farming, among others—that served the Bay Area and (soon enough) the world.

During this massive transformation of California from frontier to economic engine, there were fortunes to be made—big or small—in a million different ways. But most were made steadily, if quickly, rather than in a fortuitous choice of a spot to dig for gold. And the biggest tended to be made in real estate and trade.

That is why Thomas Larkin became one of (or perhaps the) richest man in California. It's why Faxon Atherton became nearly as rich while living in Chile for the first 12 years of the Gold Rush. It's why the financiers of the Panama Railway, and after them the financiers of the Transcontinental Railway, enjoyed some of the highest profits ever seen in their time.

Connecting this new economic engine of California to the rest of the world—and breaking it out of its isolation—was incredibly profitable.

A gold rush is never really about the gold. It's about the people it attracts. That is the real source of wealth: the ambitious, striving individuals lured by gold who ultimately turn their energies to creating civilization.

Australian Gold Rush

The gold rushes in the second half of the 19th century would completely change the face of Australia. Before 1851, Australia's combined white population was approximately 77,000. Most of those had been convicts sent by ship over the previous seventy years.

The gold rush completely changed that however. In the two years that followed Edward Hargraves's discovery at Bathurst, Australia's population increased to over 540,000. 370,000 immigrants arrived in Australia's ports during the year 1852 alone.

The flow of convicts to Australia's shores stopped. It suddenly seemed like a foolish idea (and indeed no longer a punishment) to give a free boat ride to Australia's rich gold fields to anyone who had committed a crime.

Victoria

Victoria had only been formed as a separate colony six months before the finds in Bathurst. When the first gold rush began in New South Wales, Victoria's economy slumped. Thousands of Victorian workers went north, leaving behind empty farms and industries.

A task group was formed in Melbourne known as the Gold Discovery Committee with the purpose of finding gold within the struggling colony's borders. An announcement from the committee stated that a reward of 200 pounds would be paid to anyone who found gold within 200 miles of Melbourne.

Hundreds of prospectors accepted the challenge and headed out into the rugged Victorian hills hoping to claim the reward and (just as important or perhaps more so) find gold. Despite this and the fact that over the next few months some of the richest gold fields the world has ever seen were discovered, Victoria's economic woes were not over.

In fact they only got worse. A powerfully disruptive hysteria seemed to grip the State along with the rest of the country. Farmhands simply left their employers with harvests they could no longer reap and thousands of workers fled Melbourne leaving empty industries in their wake.

Wages tripled due to scarce labour. To raise money, many property owners put their houses on the market. But as there was no one interested in buying, house prices collapsed. Due to the high wages and strained businesses, prices in most commodities rose sharply contributing to a high inflation rate.

Luckily however, this was not to last. Gold was flowing in from the incredibly rich fields of central Victoria (174 tonnes of gold worth 14,000,000 pounds in 1852 alone) and immigrants came in ridiculous numbers from Europe and China. These extra workers soon picked up the jobs that had been abandoned and were paid very highly for their effort.

And of course, lucky miners returning from the gold fields spent extravagantly easing the pressure on the suffering Melbourne.

The incredible wealth that poured out of Victoria was unthinkable. When the ships returned to England carrying eight tonnes of Australia gold, the London Times declared in 1852: "this is California all over again, but, it would appear, California on a larger scale"

"When the first reports of gold in the colonies were published in English newspapers late in 1851, few took much notice. Many dismissed them as either false or greatly exaggerated. But as the reports persisted, and especially those of fabulous finds at Mount Alexander, interest increased. It reached fever pitch when, in the middle of 1852, six ships from Victoria arrived, bringing eight tonnes of gold. The Australian colonies were the talk of London and of many other towns, as thousands hurried to get passages on southward-bound ships." R. Coupe

This wealth brought many imports and improvements to Australia. Due to the huge flow of traffic now moving around Victoria and New South Wales, the first railway was constructed. Thriving towns like Ballarat & Bendigo built libraries and roads.

All this extra money moving around brought criminals too. Theft, murder and armed robbery were common on the roads between diggings. This is the backdrop for Australia's famous bushranger past.

Incredibly, Victoria alone produced more than a third of the world's gold produced in the 1850's. By 1871 the population of Australia had increased from 540,000 to a whopping 1.7 million.

Queensland

Queensland was the next State to join in the gold rushes of the 1800's. Queensland first separated from New South Wales as a independent colony in 1959. However it was after much of the booms in New South Wales and Victoria that the State became known as a popular destination for miners.

Gold had actually been found there as early as 1858, in a township named Canoona , which caused quite a stir. A prospector known as Chapple found gold there in July and the news was widely publicised. Thousands of miners heard the call and left the heavily worked fields in Victoria and headed north. Many threw caution into the wind and spent all their savings on a passage to Canoona with high hopes.

However, the reports hadn't let on that there was only enough gold there for a few hundred diggers. When the hopeful multitudes arrived there via Rockhampton, the area was in chaos.

The tiny settlement was now overflowing with prospectors. There was nowhere near enough food to feed them all and prices exploded. Tent cities had appeared all over the landscape but little gold was to be found. Many walked away with nothing except for a hard lesson learnt.

It took over a decade before any truly profitable fields were discovered in Queensland. The first was Gympie which was a small agricultural town 160 kilometres north of Brisbane. A man named James Nash found gold in 1867 and triggered the Gympie Gold Rush. Queensland was in the grip of a crushing depression at the time and James Nash's find perhaps saved the entire colony from bankruptcy.

The event was so welcome it is still celebrated today in the week long Gympie Gold Rush Festival.

On Christmas eve 1871, a 12 year old aboriginal boy found gold in a creek at the base of Towers Hill (about 137 kilometres inland and south west of Townsville) by accident.

His name was Jupiter Mosman and he was travelling with a group of prospectors who were searching the area. Legend has it that a bolt of lightning scared their horses from their camp. While searching, Jupiter not only found the nervous mounts, but also a nugget of gold in the creek.

The rush to the area was as swift as the first diggers arriving in March. A camp had been quickly set up known as Mosman Camp but that swiftly grew into a small town with shopkeepers, blacksmiths and butchers. After that the town boomed as the gold kept flowing.

Twenty five years after the discovery, 20,000 people called the area home. The township, known as Charters Towers, is still alive today despite the fact the mining eventually dried up in the early 1900's. This mining activity has since re-started in modern times due to the reemergence of gold.

The Charters Towers goldfield still carries off the title of richest Australian gold mine. Most of the gold was concentrated into rich veins of up to 34 grams per ton. That's double what was seen in Victoria and 75% higher than that of Kalgoorlie, Western Australia.

Mount Morgan, Rockhampton was another famous Queensland gold mine. It began work in 1882 and closed in 1981. One man, William Knox D'Arcy, made a fortune at Mount Morgan and reinvested in oil exploration in Iran. His company was known as the Anglo-Persian Oil Company but now exists today as British Petroleum (BP).

Western Australia

The great western state was slow to join in on the booms of the east due to rugged terrain, harsh climates and its sheer distance from the heavily populated areas of Sydney and Melbourne. However, with most of the easy gold already gone and the eastern states in the grip of a economic depression during the late 1800's, Western Australia finally got its golden age.

Gold was first discovered officially in Western Australia (WA) in 1892 by William Ford and Arthur Bailey at Fly Flat (a previous name for modern Coolgardie). Bailey reported he had mined 554 ounces of gold and received a 20 acre reward claim. This was worked until 1963 yielding 500,000 ounces of gold.

Due to the crushing depression in the east, especially in the older mining regions in Victoria, many travelled to Coolgardie hoping for an easier life. However, they were unprepared for the difficult challenges WA's environment had in store for them.

Mining in Victoria or New South Wales was a far more simple task. The sun was hot was but water was not too hard to come by. Food was closer and could be found in the bush if a digger was wise. Western Australia however was mostly desert.

Water and food were very scarce and extremely expensive to transport into the savage wilderness of the west. Hundreds of diggers who came unprepared would suffer disease, dehydration, heat stroke and many died. Despite these hardships, the allure of gold was too powerful and miners continued to arrive in the thousands.

Incredibly, it only took ten years for Coolgardie's population to rise to 16,000. By 1896, the first railway had arrived allowing for much easier (and cheaper) transport. The town continued to grow and in 1898, Coolgardie had become the 3rd largest town in Western Australia behind Perth and Fremantle.

Coolgardie is thought by many to be the mother of Western Australian goldfields.

The next big find was Kalgoorlie. A trio of Irish gold prospectors found gold near Mount Charlotte in 1893. Those three lucky diggers were named Paddy Hannan, Tom Flannagan and Dan Shea. News travelled very swiftly and soon hundreds were arriving into the hastily erected camp known as Hannan's Find.

Many of the diggers came from nearby Coolgardie, distracted from the gold fields there in a similar fashion to other discoveries in the eastern states decades earlier. However, a great many poured in from the economically weakened east and across the southern deserts hoping to make their fortune.

The area was later named Kalgoorlie which is derived from an Aboriginal word meaning "place of the silky pears". By 1903, Kalgoorlie had a population of 30,000.

After these finds, many more were discovered north and south of the Kalgoorlie-Coolgardie region. Gold prospecting became the topic in almost every conversation in Perth and around the state. Despite the harsh sun and lack of available water, explorers and prospectors scoured the land for new deposits.

In 1894, a man named Laurie Sinclair found gold in the Dundas area (south of Kalgoorlie). He named the find Norseman after his own horse, 'Hardy Norseman'. That mine still exists today as Australia's longest lasting gold mine operation.

Up north, the Leonora deposit and the Youanmi gold find in Murchison were discovered. Gold mining became more organised. Hundreds of companies were floated on the London stock exchange. This shadowed the end of the digger working a small 3.6 square metre claim and foretold of the future's mining conglomerates.

Many of the gold fields in Western Australia (as well as the rest of the country) had the majority of their gold buried far below what miners could uncover with pan and shovel. Later, smaller gold rushes have occurred when mining techniques improved and gold is still found in many of these regions today.

What Moves Gold

As one of the oldest currencies on the planet, gold has embedded itself deeply into the psyche of the financial world. Nearly everyone has an opinion about the yellow metal, but gold itself reacts only to a limited number of price catalysts. Each of these forces splits down the middle in a polarity that impacts sentiment, volume and trend intensity:

Inflation and deflation

Greed and fear

Supply and demand

Market players face elevated risk when they trade gold in reaction to one of these polarities, when in fact it's another one controlling price action. For example, say a selloff hits world financial markets, and gold takes off in a strong rally. Many traders assume that fear is moving the yellow metal and jump in, believing the emotional crowd will blindly carry price higher. However, inflation may have actually triggered the stock's decline, attracting a more technical crowd that will sell against the gold rally aggressively.

Combinations of these forces are always in play in world markets, establishing long-term themes that track equally long uptrends and downtrends. For example, the Federal Reserve (FOMC) economic stimulus begun in 2009, initially had little effect on gold because market players were focused on high fear levels coming out of the 2008 economic collapse. However, this quantitative easing encouraged deflation, setting up the gold market and other commodity groups for a major reversal.

That turnaround didn't happen immediately because a reflation bid was underway, with depressed financial and commodity-based assets spiraling back toward historical means. Gold finally topped out and turned lower in 2011 after reflation was completed and central banks intensified their quantitative easing policies.

2. Understand the Crowd

Gold attracts numerous crowds with diverse and often opposing interests. Gold bugs stand at the top of the heap, collecting physical bullion and allocating an outsized portion of family assets to gold equities, options, and futures. These are long-term players, rarely dissuaded by downtrends, who eventually shake out less ideological players. In addition, retail participants comprise nearly the entire population of gold bugs, with few funds devoted entirely to the long side of the precious metal.

In addition, gold attracts enormous hedging activity by institutional investors who buy and sell in combination with currencies and bonds in bilateral strategies known as "risk-on" and risk-off." Funds create baskets of instruments matching growth (risk-on) and safety (risk-off), trading these combinations through lightning-fast algorithms. They are especially popular in highly conflicted markets in which public participation is lower than normal.

Gold Monthly Chart

Take time to learn the gold chart inside and out, starting with a long-term history that goes back at least 100 years. In addition to carving out trends that persisted for decades, the metal has also trickled lower for incredibly long periods

Gold's recent history shows little movement until the 1970s, when following the removal of the gold standard for the dollar, it took off in a long uptrend, underpinned by rising inflation due to skyrocketing crude oil prices. After topping out at $2,076 an ounce in February 1980, it turned lower near $700 in the mid-1980s, in reaction to restrictive Federal Reserve monetary policy.

The subsequent downtrend lasted into the late 1990s when gold entered the historic uptrend that culminated in the February 2012 top of $1,916 an ounce. A steady decline since that time has relinquished around 700 points in four years; although in the first quarter of 2016 it surged 17% for its biggest quarterly gain in three decades, as of December 2017, it's trading at $1,267 per ounce.

Liquidity follows gold trends, increasing when it's moving sharply higher or lower and decreasing during relatively quiet periods. This oscillation impacts the futures markets to a greater degree than it does equity markets, due to much lower average participation rates.

Bottom Line

Trade the gold market profitably in four steps. First, learn how three polarities impact the majority of gold buying and selling decisions. Second, familiarize yourself with the diverse crowds that focus on gold trading, hedging, and ownership. Third, take time to analyze the long and short-term gold charts, with an eye on key price levels that may come into play.

Finally, choose your venue for risk-taking, focused on high liquidity and easy trade execution.

Importance of gold and trade

Throughout history, gold has been highly valued for coinage, jewelry and the arts. Gold is considered a unique store of value and the symbol of power, strength and wealth. Since April 2001 it has more than quintupled in value.

Throughout history, gold has been highly valued for coinage, jewelry and the arts. Gold is considered a unique store of value and the symbol of power, strength and wealth. Since April 2001 it has more than quintupled in value.

The poet Virgil describes man's underlying lust for gold when he wrote "Auri Sacra Fames" (the accursed thirst for gold). In the 19th century, gold mining expanded around the world with the 1848 California gold rush which helped the settlement of the American West. In 1869, South Africa became a major source of the world's gold after the discovery of the Witwatersrand basin and the Canadian Yukon gold rush followed in 1896.

Approximately 65% of all the gold in the world has been mined since 1950 and the finite supply of gold adds to its rarity and attraction. But how did it all begin?

Various forms of livestock, in particular cattle, and grains were the earliest forms used to settle trades and payment for good goods and services. Cattle are hard to carry in your pocket and grains spoil so an alternative currency was needed.

In 560 BC, the Greek state of Lydia in Asia Minor introduced the first gold coins. The use of gold coins as currency spread quickly throughout the Mediterranean and Middle East regions. The Romans mined gold extensively and Venice introduced the gold "Ducat" which became the most popular coin in the world for the next 500 years. In 19th century America, a movement to use silver coins and adopt a bimetallic monetary system emerged. The US Congress did not authorise the printing of paper money until 1861.

For most of the early 20th century, Americans were forbidden to buy or trade gold. In 1946, the Bretton Woods agreement fixed the price of gold at $35 an ounce, creating a gold standard and the US dollar (USD) became backed by gold. A gold standard is defined as a monetary system in which the standard economic unit of account is a fixed mass of gold.

The Bretton Woods agreement of fixed exchange rates was implemented to combat deflationary pressures, economic dislocations and currency instability which emerged after World War I and II. Soon after the agreement was signed, the USD became the world's reserve currency.

In the following years, there were significant strains on the system of fixed exchange rates as the US balance of payments with the rest of the world grew dramatically. Foreign central banks exercised their gold convertibility rights causing a sharp decline in US gold reserves.

In 1971, the Bretton Woods system was abandoned when there was no longer enough gold to cover all the paper money in circulation. The USD became a "fiat" currency backed by nothing more than the health of the US economy and the promise of the US government. A fiat currency's value is based on the issuing authority's promise to pay; not an intrinsic value or extrinsic backing. In 1974, the ban on US ownership of gold bars was lifted and US citizens were allowed to trade gold.

The end of the gold standard ushered in the current system of floating exchange rates. In 1972, the Chicago Mercantile Exchange (CME) launched futures trading in seven currencies and in 1974 the first gold futures contract was traded on the COMEX exchange in New York. The 1980's experienced a sharp expansion of over-the-counter trading in currencies and gold and the beginning of online trading.

Recently, we have seen gold prices surging to an all-time high as nations, institutions and investors seek safe haven and are using gold as a hedge against inflation and protection against losses in other assets like stocks and bonds and commodities. Investors buying gold are sometimes called "gold bugs." Gold bugs are also described as a person opposed to the use of fiat currency and are supportive of a return to the gold standard.

Unlike a fiat currency, money backed by gold cannot be created arbitrarily by government action. The supply of gold is finite and printing of paper limitless. The term gold bug is thought to have been derived from an Edgar Allen Poe poem the "Gold -bug." In the poem, two adventurers decipher a secret message that leads to a buried treasure.

Since April 2001, the price of gold has more quintupled in value and hit all-time high of $1913.50 in August 2011. The price movement in gold has been quite volatile with prices rising and falling quickly. Investors have shown high levels of interest in trading gold.

Like foreign currency (forex), trading with gold rates does not require the "physical" purchase or sale of the real material. If you buy forex gold for the price of 1850.97USD, you do not have an ounce of gold that you can hold in your pocket, but you rather have the obligation to buy gold (XAU) at $1850.97. When you close your forex deal, you sell the gold and close your obligation. If you sell it for the price of $1853.00, you have made a profit of $2.03 for every ounce (unit) of gold in your contract.

Rising gold prices can also affect other currencies. Higher gold prices can be especially important to the currencies of major gold-producing countries. Australia, Canada and South Africa are all large producers of gold, so if you believe the price of gold will continue to rise, you can establish trades in the Australian dollar (AUD), the Canadian dollar (CAD) or the South African Rand (ZAR) because those currencies may become stronger.

It may be wise to keep an eye on gold prices when the international political or economic situation is changing, such as during times when global inflation is rising. If the gold price starts to increase, you might expect it to go higher in the next periods of trading.

Owning gold

While you don't eat it or drink it, people are attracted to gold. It's been used as a currency because it doesn't corrode, and the material allows for some absorption of light creating that yellow glow. The value of gold fluctuates from moment to moment, as it is now traded on public exchanges where it's price is determined by supply and demand.

The reasons people buy or sell gold--creating the demand and supply respectively--may be pure speculation, acquiring or distributing physical gold, hedging or commercial application. For day traders, the purpose of trading gold is to profit from its price movements.

Futures Markets

Day trading gold is speculating on its short-term price movements. Physical gold is not actually handled or taken possession of, rather the transactions take place electronically and only profits or losses are reflected in the trading account.

There are a few ways to trade gold. The main way is through a futures contract. A futures contract is an agreement to buy or sell something--like gold--at a future date. Buying a gold futures contract doesn't mean you have to take possession of the physical commodity.

Day traders close out all contracts (trades) each day, and make a profit based on the difference between the price they bought the contract and the price they sold it at. Gold futures trade on the Chicago Mercantile Exchange (CME). There is standard gold future (GC) which represents 100 troy ounces of gold, and a micro gold future (MGC), which represents 10 troy ounces.

On the futures exchange, gold moves in $0.10 increments only. This increment is called a "tick"--it is the smallest movement a futures contract can make. If you buy or sell a futures contract, how many ticks the price moves away from your entry price determines your profit or loss. To calculate your profit or loss (your trading platform will also show you, but it is good to understand how it works) you'll first need to know the tick value of the contract you are trading.

For a standard contract the tick value is $10. This is because the contract represents 100 ounces of gold, and 100 ounces multiplied by the $0.10 tick size results in $10. That means for each contract, a one tick movement will result in a profit or loss of $10. If it moves 10 ticks, you win or loss $100. If it moves 10 ticks and you are holding 3 contracts, your profit or loss is $300.

For a micro contract the tick value is $1. This is because the contract represents 10 ounces of gold, and 10 ounces multiplied by the $0.10 tick size results in $1. That means for each contract, a one tick movement will result in a profit or loss of $1. If it moves 10 ticks, you win or loss $10. If it moves 10 ticks and you are holding 3 contracts, your profit or loss is $30.

Gold Futures

The amount you need in your account to day trade a gold futures contract will depend on your futures broker. Vcykev Brokers for examples requires you have $500 in your account to open a position for one E-Micro Gold Futures (MGC) contract. You also need enough in the account to accommodate for potential losses (need much more than $500).

To day trade a standard Gold Futures (GC) contract, you need $1000 in your account, plus additional funds to accommodate losses. The amount required by your broker to open a day trading position is called Intra-day margin; it varies by the broker and is subject to change.

These figures assume you are day trading and closing out positions before the market closes each day. If you hold positions overnight, you are subject to Initial Margin and Maintenance Margin requirements, which will require you have more money in your account.

Day Trading Gold, ETFs and/or Stock Market

Another way to day trade gold is through a fund which trades on a stock exchange, like the SPDR Gold Trust (GLD). If you have a stock trading account, you can trade the price movements in gold.

The trust holds gold in reserve, and therefore, its value is reflective of the price of gold. The price of the SPDR Gold Trust is approximately 1/10 of the price of gold. So if gold futures are trading at $1500, then the Gold Trust will trade at approximately $150.

The trust trades like any stock. The minimum price movement is $0.01, therefore you make or lose $0.01 for each share you own each time the price changes by a penny. Stocks and ETFs are typically traded in 100 share blocks (called lots) so if the price moves a penny and you are holding 100 shares, you make or lose $1.

If the price moves $1, from $120 to $121, you make or lose $100 on your 100 share position. If you are holding 500 shares, you make or lose $500 on that same price move. The amount you need in your account to day trade a gold ETF depends on the price of the ETF, your leverage, and position size.

To day trade stocks or ETFs in the US, you're required to have a $25,000 minimum balance in your account. Depending on how much income you want to generate and your leverage, you may wish to have more than $25,000 available to you.

How to Buy Gold Bullion

In today's turbulent economy, investors must diversify their assets in order to mitigate the potential downside risks associated with individual components of their investment portfolio. Within each of the four key investment classes – cash, securities, real estate and tangible assets – one should look critically at the trends and potential risks inherent to each investment class.

Financial advisors have long recommended portfolio diversification with hard assets such as precious metals for better portfolio returns over time. As one of the only forms of real, lasting wealth, gold is a classic, time-tested hedge against economic uncertainty, inflation, deflation and geo-political risk. Gold is easy to buy, sell and store, and is recognized and accepted worldwide. Gold, and gold bullion, is the ultimate on-shore asset that remains off the balance sheet.

Buying Physical Gold Bullion Bars

Purchasing gold bullion bars can be an effective method to acquire gold assets at a relatively low cost per troy-ounce of the metal. When purchasing gold bullion bars, it is important to understand that gold bars are available for purchase in many different sizes. Gold bullion bars are available in standard 1-troy ounce, 10-troy ounce and 32.15-troy ounce (or "kilo-bar") sizes, as well as in larger 100-ounce and 400-ounce bar sizes. Smaller gold bars, weighing less than one-troy ounce, are also available from some dealers. Gold ingots are generally pure gold, with an industry standard minimum fineness of .995 fine, ensuring the highest quality, purity and clarity.

Gold bullion bar prices generally include a small premium over the spot gold price to cover the manufacturing costs of the bar. As a general rule, the larger the gold bar, the smaller the premium in percentage terms. So to ensure that an investor pays the lowest premium possible, gold bars should be purchased in the largest possible size.

As with any investment, knowing the background and legitimacy of the gold dealer you are investing with is of the utmost importance. Established dealers offer gold bars that are refined and produced by recognized manufacturers and refiners, offering some protection against counterfeiting. Additionally, investors should expect to pay an assay fee when buying or selling gold bullion through a dealer to ensure the purity and authenticity of the asset. These assay checks determine the legitimacy of the metal, assuring the safety of both parties.

When purchasing and selling gold bullion it is important to understand that the transactions are taxable events. You should consult a tax professional to determine how your personal tax liability could be impacted.

Additional Ways to Purchase Gold

As an alternative to investing in gold through the purchase of gold bullion bars, gold bullion coins offer another way to own pure gold bullion that is easy to buy, hold, divide and trade. Gold bullion coins are issued by government mints and are legal tender in the country in which they are produced, and thus, the coins' face value, metal purity and metal content associated with your gold coin investment are guaranteed. Most modern gold bullion coin issues contain exactly 1-oz, ½-oz, ¼-oz or 1/10-oz of pure gold in each coin, while older issues contain other fractional amounts of pure gold. As a result, older issue gold bullion coins tend to be more difficult to price.

For more information; bichangakevin@gmail.com

1845 annexation of Texas: the incorporation of the Republic of Texas into the United States of America. In 1836 the Texian Army won the Battle of San Jacinto against Mexican forces, led by famed general Santa Anna, and the Republic of Texas declared its independence from Mexico. But Mexico had refused to acknowledge this action and warned the U.S. that if it tried to make Texas part of the U.S., Mexico would declare war. In 1845 Texas voluntarily asked to join the U.S., and became the 28th state. This action led to Mexico to declare war on the United States, starting the Mexican-American War.

forty-niners: people, especially prospectors, who went to California in 1849 during the gold rush.

Henry David Thoreau: (1817-1862) American author and poet, best known for his work Walden (1854), a novel that is both memoir, social experiment, and a voyage of spiritual discovery. It is a reflection of a man's experience living simply in nature, outside "civilized" society.

John Sutter: (1803-1880) German-born Swiss settler and colonizer of California. The discovery of gold on his land at Sutter's Mill precipitated the California Gold Rush.

Klondike Gold Rush: (1896-1899) a migration by approximately 100,000 prospectors to the Klondike region of the Yukon in north-western Canada. Similar to the California Gold Rush, while the very first prospectors did find gold, most found their search in vain.

Manifest Destiny: the nineteenth-century doctrine or belief that the expansion of the U.S. throughout the American continents was both justified and inevitable.

Mexican Cession: the historical name for the region of the United States that Mexico ceded to the U.S. in the Treaty of Guadalupe-Hidalgo in 1848.

Ralph Waldo Emerson: (1803-1882) American poet, essayist, and philosopher; founder of the Transcendentalist philosophical movement.

Santa Anna: (Antonio López de Santa Anna) (1794-1876) influential Mexican military and political leader, best known for his victory at the Battle of the Alamo in 1836.

Sutter's Mill: the water-powered saw mill owned by John Sutter, where gold was discovered in

1848, setting off the California Gold Rush. It was located in present-day Coloma, California on the bank of the South Fork American River.

References

"Gold standard Facts, information, pictures Encyclopedia.com articles about Gold standard". www.encyclopedia.com. Retrieved 2015-12-05.

William O. Scroggs. "What Is Left of the Gold Standard?". foreignaffairs.com. Retrieved 28 January 2015.

"Gold Standard". IGM Forum. 12 January 2012. Retrieved 27 December 2015.

Appelbaum, Binyamin (2015-12-01). "G.O.P. Candidates Viewing Economy's Past Through Gold-Colored Glasses". The New York Times. ISSN 0362-4331. Retrieved 2017-07-20.

Lipsey 1975, pp. 683-702.

Bordo, Dittmar & Gavin 2003 "in a world with two capital goods, the one with the lower depreciation rate emerges as commodity money"

"World's Oldest Coin - First Coins". rg.ancients.info. Retrieved 2015-12-05.

Lopez, Robert Sabatino (Summer 1951). "The Dollar of the Middle Ages". The Journal of Economic History. 11 (3): 209–234. doi:10.1017/s0022050700084746. JSTOR 2113933.

Keary, Charles Francis. (2005). A Catalogue of English Coins in the British Museum. Anglo-Saxon Series. Volume I. Poole, Reginald Stewart, ed. Elibron Classics. pp. ii, xxii–xxv

Rothwell, Richard Pennefather. (1893). Universal Bimetallism and An International Monetary Clearing House, together with A Record of the World's Money, Statistics of Gold and Silver, Etc. New York: The Scientific Publishing Company. pp. 45.

Andrei, Liviu C. (2011). Money and Market in the Economy of All Times: Another World History of Money and Pre-Money Based Economies. Xlibris Corporation. pp. 146–147.

James Powell, A History of the Canadian Dollar (Ottawa: Bank of Canada, 2005), pp. 22-23, 33.

Consolidated Statutes of Newfoundland (1st Series, 1874), Title XXV, "Of the Regulation of Trade in Certain Cases", c. 92, Of the Currency, s. 8.

"Small change". UK Parliament. Retrieved 2019-02-09.

Walton & Rockoff 2010.

Metzler, Mark (2006). Lever of Empire: The International Gold Standard and the Crisis of Liberalism in Prewar Japan. Berkeley: University of California Press. ISBN 978-0-520-24420-7.

Elwell 2011.

Friedman & Schwartz 1963, p. 79.

Kemmerer, Edwin Walter (1994). Gold and the Gold Standard: The Story of Gold Money Past, Present and Future. Princeton, NJ: McGraw-Hill Book, Company, Inc. pp. 154 (238 pg). ISBN 9781610164429.

Nicholson, J. S. (April 1915). "The Abandonment of the Gold Standard". The Quarterly Review. 223: 409–423.

Officer

Eichengreen 1995.

Drummond, Ian M. The Gold Standard and the International Monetary System 1900–1939. Macmillan Education, LTD, 1987.

"Gold Standard Act 1925 1.c.2".

"Articles: Free the Planet: Gold Standard Act 1925". Free the Planet. 2009-06-10. Archived from the original on 2012-07-13. Retrieved 2012-07-09.

Keynes, John Maynard (1920). Economic Consequences of the Peace. New York: Harcourt, Brace and Rowe.

"Thatcher warned Major about exchange rate risks before ERM crisis". The Guardian. 2017-12-29. Retrieved 2017-12-29.

Cassel, Gustav. The Downfall of the Gold Standard. Oxford University Press, 1936.

"Chancellor's Commons Speech". Freetheplanet.net. Archived from the original on 2012-07-09. Retrieved 2012-07-09.

Eichengreen, Barry J. (September 15, 2008). Globalizing Capital: A History of the International Monetary System. Princeton University Press. pp. 61–. ISBN 978-0-691-13937-1. Retrieved November 23, 2010.

Officer, Lawrence. "Breakdown of the Interwar Gold Standard". Eh.net. Archived from the original on November 24, 2005. Retrieved 2012-07-09.

Officer, Lawrence. "there was ongoing tension with France, that resented the sterling-dominated gold-exchange standard and desired to cash in its sterling holding for gold to aid its objective of achieving first-class financial status for Paris". Eh.net. Archived from the original on November 24, 2005. Retrieved 2012-07-09.

International data from Maddison, Angus. "Historical Statistics for the World Economy: 1–2003 AD".[permanent dead link]. Gold dates culled from historical sources, principally Eichengreen, Barry (1992). Golden Fetters: The Gold Standard and the Great Depression, 1919–1939. New York: Oxford University Press. ISBN 978-0-19-506431-5.

Eichengreen 1995, Preface.

American Economic Association (2000–2011). "The Elasticity of the Federal Reserve Note". The American Economic Review. ITHAKA. 26 (4): 683–690. JSTOR 1807996.

"Remarks by Governor Ben S. Bernanke At the Conference to Honor Milton Friedman". The Federal Reserve Board. November 8, 2002. Retrieved December 24, 2011.

Friedman & Schwartz 1963, p. 543.

Friedman & Schwartz 1963, p. 544.

"FRB: Speech, Bernanke-Money, Gold, and the Great Depression – March 2, 2004". Federalreserve.gov. 2004-03-02. Retrieved 2010-07-24.

"1931—"The Tragic Year"". Ludwig von Mises Institute. Retrieved December 24, 2011. The inflationary attempts of the government from January to October were thus offset by the people's attempts to convert their bank deposits into legal tender" "Hence, the will of the public caused bank reserves to decline by $400 million in the latter half of 1931, and the money supply, as a consequence, fell by over four billion dollars in the same period.

"1931—"The Tragic Year"". Ludwig von Mises Institute. Retrieved December 24, 2011. Throughout the European crisis, the Federal Reserve, particularly the New York Bank, tried its best to aid the European governments and to prop up unsound credit positions. ... The New York Federal Reserve loaned, in 1931, $125 million to the Bank of England, $25 million to the German Reichsbank, and smaller amounts to Hungary and Austria. As a result, much frozen assets were shifted, to become burdens to the United States.

"In the 1930s, the United States was in a situation that satisfied the conditions for a liquidity trap. Over 1929–1933 overnight rates fell to zero, and they remained on the floor through the 1930's" (PDF). Archived from the original on 2004-07-22.

The European Economy between Wars; Feinstein, Temin, and Toniolo

Dominic Sandbrook (2011-12-31). "In August 1932, the British colonies and dominions met in the Canadian capital, Ottawa, and agreed a policy of Imperial Preference, putting high tariffs on goods from outside the Empire". London: Dailymail.co.uk. Retrieved 2012-07-09.

M. Friedman "the severity of each of the major contractions – 1920–21, 1929–33 and 1937–38 is directly attributable to acts of commission and omission by the Reserve authorities".

Robert P. Murphy. "Another major factor is that governments in the 1930s were interfering with wages and prices more so than at any prior point in (peacetime) history". Mises.org. Retrieved 2012-07-09.

"High Taxes and High Budget Deficits-The Hoover–Roosevelt Tax Increases of the 1930s" (PDF).

"per data from Economics Professor Mark J. Perry". Mjperry.blogspot.com. 2008-11-09. Retrieved 2012-07-09.

Eichengreen, Barry; Mitchener, Kris (August 2003). "The Great Depression as a Credit Boom Gone Wrong" (PDF). Retrieved December 24, 2011.

Gold and Economic Freedom by Alan Greenspan 1966 "Great Britain fared even worse, and rather than absorb the full consequences of her previous folly, she abandoned the gold standard completely in 1931, tearing asunder what remained of the fabric of confidence and inducing a world-wide series of bank failures."

Farrell, Paul B. (December 13, 2011). "Our decade from hell will get worse in 2012". MarketWatch. Retrieved December 24, 2011. As financial historian Niall Ferguson writes in Newsweek: "Double-Dip Depression ... We forget that the Great Depression was like a soccer match, there were two halves." The

1929 crash kicked off the first half. But what "made the depression truly 'great' ... began with the European banking crisis of 1931." Sound familiar?

Aftershock by Robert B. Reich, published 2010 Chapter 1 Eccles's Insight.

Prior, Ed (1 April 2013). "How much gold is there in the world?" – via www.bbc.com.

"FAQs | Investment | World Gold Council". Gold.org. Retrieved 2013-09-12.

"Measuring Worth - GDP result".

"Download entire World Economic Outlook database, April 2013".

Krech, Shepard; John Robert McNeill; Carolyn Merchant (2004). Encyclopedia of world environmental history. New York City: Routledge. p. 597. ISBN 978-0-415-93734-4. OCLC 174950341.

Bernanke, Ben (March 2, 2004), "Remarks by Governor Ben S. Bernanke: Money, Gold and the Great Depression", At the H. Parker Willis Lecture in Economic Policy, Washington and Lee University, Lexington, Virginia.

Hoppe, Hans-Herman (1992). Mark Skousen, ed. Dissent on Keynes, A Critical Appraisal of Economics. pp. 199–223.

"Gold as Money: FAQ". Mises.org. Ludwig von Mises Institute. Archived from the original on July 14, 2011. Retrieved 12 August 2011.

The New Palgrave Dictionary of Economics, 2nd edition (2008), Vol.3, S.695

Bordo 2008.

"Advantages of the Gold Standard" (PDF). The Gold Standard: Perspectives in the Austrian School. The Ludwig von Mises Institute. Retrieved 9 January 2011.

Ransom, Roger L. (February 1, 2010). "The Economics of the Civil War". Economic History Association. Archived from the original on December 13, 2011. Retrieved December 24, 2011. the Union also experienced inflation as a result of deficit finance during the war; the consumer price index rose from 100 at the outset of the war to 175 by the end of 1865

Whaples, Robert (February 5, 2010). "California Gold Rush". Economic History Association. Archived from the original on November 24, 2011. Retrieved December 24, 2011. from 1792 until 1847 cumulative U.S. production of gold was only about 37 tons. California's production in 1849 alone exceeded this figure, and annual production from 1848 to 1857 averaged 76 tons. ... Soaring gold output from the California and Australia gold rushes is linked with a 30 percent increase in wholesale prices from 1850 through 1855

"Why the Gold Standard Is the World's Worst Economic Idea, in 2 Charts – Matthew O'Brien". The Atlantic. 2012-08-26. Retrieved 2013-04-19.

"Reform of the International Monetary and Financial System" (PDF). Bank of England. December 2011. Archived from the original (PDF) on December 18, 2011. Retrieved December 24, 2011. Countries with current account surpluses accumulated gold, while deficit countries saw their gold stocks diminish. This, in turn, contributed to upward pressure on domestic spending and prices in surplus countries and downward pressure on them in deficit countries, thereby leading to a change ... that should, eventually, have reduced imbalances.

"Financial Repression Redux". International Monetary Fund. June 2011. Retrieved December 24, 2011. Financial repression occurs when governments implement policies to channel to themselves funds that in a deregulated market environment would go elsewhere

Reinhart, Carmen M.; Rogoff, Kenneth S. (2008). This Time is Different. Princeton University Press. p. 143.

Giovannini, Alberto; De Melo, Martha (1993). "Government Revenue from Financial Repression". The American Economic Review. 83 (4): 953–963. JSTOR 2117587.

Greenspan, Alan (1966). "Gold and Economic Freedom". Constitution.org. Retrieved December 24, 2011.

Goodman, George J.W., Paper Money, 1981, p. 165–6

Hill, Liezel (January 13, 2011). "Gold mine output hit record in 2010, more gains likely this year – GFMS". Mining Weekly. Retrieved December 24, 2011.

U.S. Geological Survey (January 2011). "GOLD" (PDF). U.S. Geological Survey, Mineral Commodity Summaries. U.S. Department of the Interior | U.S. Geological Survey. Retrieved 10 July 2012.

Mayer, David A. Gold standard at Google Books The Everything Economics Book: From theory to practice, your complete guide to understanding economics today (Everything Series) ISBN 978-1-4405-0602-4. 2010. pp. 33–34.

Mankiw, N. Gregory (2002). Macroeconomics (5th ed.). Worth. pp. 238–255. ISBN 978-0-324-17190-7.

Krugman, Paul. "The Gold Bug Variations". Slate.com. Retrieved 2009-02-13.

Timberlake, Richard H. (2005). "Gold Standards and the Real Bills Doctrine in US Monetary Policy". Econ Journal Watch. 2 (2): 196–233.

Bordo, Dittmar & Gavin 2003.

Keogh, Bryan (May 13, 2009). "Real Rate Shock Hits CEOs as Borrowing Costs Impede Recovery". Bloomberg. Retrieved December 24, 2011. Deflation hurts borrowers and rewards savers," said Drew Matus, senior economist at Banc of America Securities-Merrill Lynch in New York, in a telephone interview. "If you do borrow right now, and we go through a period of deflation, your cost of borrowing just went through the roof.

Mauldin, John; Tepper, Jonathan (2011-02-09). Endgame: The End of the Debt SuperCycle and How It Changes Everything. Hoboken, N.J.: John Wiley. ISBN 978-1-118-00457-9.

"The greater of two evils". The Economist. May 7, 2009. Retrieved December 24, 2011.

DeLong, Brad (1996-08-10). "Why Not the Gold Standard?". Berkeley, California: University of California, Berkeley. Retrieved 2008-09-25.

Warburton, Clark (1966). "The Monetary Disequilibrium Hypothesis". Depression, Inflation, and Monetary Policy: Selected Papers, 1945–1953. Baltimore: Johns Hopkins University Press. pp. 25–35. OCLC 736401.

Hamilton 2005.

Hamilton 1988.

Christina D. Romer (20 December 2003). "Great Depression" (PDF). ELSA. University of California Regents. Archived from the original (PDF) on 14 December 2011. Retrieved 10 July 2012.

"Remarks by Governor Ben S. Bernanke". The Federal Reserve Board. March 2, 2004. Retrieved December 24, 2011. "In September 1931, following a period of financial upheaval in Europe that created concerns about British investments on the Continent, speculators attacked the British pound, presenting pounds to the Bank of England and demanding gold in return. ... Unable to continue supporting the pound at its official value, Great Britain was forced to leave the gold standard, ... With the collapse of the pound, speculators turned their attention to the U.S. dollar

McArdle, Megan (2007-09-04). "There's gold in them thar standards!". The Atlantic Monthly. Retrieved 2008-11-12.

Hummel, Jeffrey Rogers. "Death and Taxes, Including Inflation: the Public versus Economists" (January 2007).[1] p.56

Demirgüç-Kunt, Asli; Enrica Detragiache (April 2005). "Cross-Country Empirical Studies of Systemic Bank Distress: A Survey". National Institute Economic Review. 192 (1): 68–83. doi:10.1177/002795010519200108. ISSN 0027-9501. OCLC 90233776. Retrieved 2008-11-12.

"the quantity of money supplied by the Fed must be equal to the quantity demanded by money holders" (PDF). Archived from the original (PDF) on June 16, 2012. Retrieved 2012-07-09.

Paul, Ron; Lewis Lehrman (1982). The case for gold: a minority report of the U.S. Gold Commission (PDF). Washington, D.C.: Cato Institute. p. 160. ISBN 978-0-932790-31-6. OCLC 8763972. Retrieved 2008-11-12.

al-'Amraawi, Muhammad; Al-Khammar al-Baqqaali; Ahmad Saabir; Al-Hussayn ibn Haashim; Abu Sayf Kharkhaash; Mubarak Sa'doun al-Mutawwa'; Malik Abu Hamza Sezgin; Abdassamad Clarke; Asadullah Yate (2001-07-01). "Declaration of 'Ulama on the Gold Dinar". Islam i Dag. Archived from the original on 2008-06-24. Retrieved 2008-11-14.

McGregor, Richard (2011-01-16). "Richard McGregor:Hu questions future role of US dollar. Financial Times, January 16, 2011". Financial Times. Retrieved December 24, 2011.

"Conduct of Monetary Policy: Report of the Federal Reserve Board Pursuant to the Full Employment and Balanced Growth Act of 1978, P.L. 95-523 and The State of the Economy : Hearing Before the Subcommittee on Domestic and International Monetary Policy of the Committee on Banking and Financial Services, House of Representatives, One Hundred Fifth Congress, Second Session, July 22, 1998 - FRASER - St. Louis Fed".

Greenspan, Alan (July 1966). "Gold and Economic Freedom". The Objectivist. 5 (7). Retrieved 2008-10-16.

Paul, Ron. End the Fed. p. xxiii.

Salerno 1982.

Boaz, David (2009-03-12). "Time to Think about the Gold Standard?". Cato Institute. Retrieved 2018-05-05.

Channel: CNBC. Show: Squawk Box. Date: 11/13/2009. Interview with Ron Paul

Clark, Stephen (March 3, 2011). "Utah Considers Return to Gold, Silver Coins". Fox News. Retrieved December 24, 2011.

CNN (2011-03-29). "Utah: Forget dollars. How about gold?".

Spillius, Alex (2011-03-18). "Tea Party legislation reveals anxiety at US direction under Barack Obama". The Daily Telegraph. London.

http://www.azleg.gov/govlettr/51leg/1R/SB1439.pdf

Appelbaum, Binyamin (2015-12-01). "The Good Old Days of the Gold Standard? Not Really, Historians Say". The New York Times. ISSN 0362-4331. Retrieved 2015-12-02.

Bowyer, Jerry (23 October 2013). "My Friendly Debate On The Gold Standard With Allan Meltzer, The World's Leading Monetarist". Forbes / Contributor Opinions. Retrieved 27 December 2015.

www.ingramcontent.com/pod-product-compliance
Lightning Source LLC
Chambersburg PA
CBHW021834170526
45157CB00007B/2805